Film Production: Theory and Practice

Stephen Hoover

Film Production: Theory and Practice

Copyright © 2013 by Stephen Hoover

Library of Congress Control Number: 2013922640

Book design by: Cat Stewart

Cover design by: 2Faced Design

All rights reserved. No part of this book may be used or reproduced in any manner whatsoever including Internet usage, without written permission of the author.

ISBN: 978-1-941084-03-8

Table of Contents

CHAPTER 1 THE SCOPE OF PRODUCING A FILM 1

FOR A MOMENT, BE PRACTICAL 1
CAN IT EVEN BE DONE? 3
GREAT SCRIPT, AWFUL ACTING, HORRIBLE CAMERA OPERATOR 4
DON'T SACRIFICE YOUR FILM TO SILLY IDEALS 5
LOVE YOUR WORK 7

CHAPTER 2 THE WORK OF PRODUCTION 9

GETTING THE RIGHTS 9
BUYING A SCRIPT 14
WRITING A SCRIPT 14
BOOKS INTO A SCRIPT 15
THE PUBLIC DOMAIN 16
TIPS FOR DEALING WITH PROPERTY OWNERS 18

CHAPTER 3 THE PREPRODUCTION PROCESS 19

FIXING THE SCRIPT 19
FINDING THE DIRECTOR 21
HIRING THE CAST 24
HIRING THE CREW 28
SETTING STANDARDS 36
COORDINATION 38
CHAIN OF COMMAND 39
MAKING TOUGH DECISIONS 39
BRINGING IT ALL TOGETHER 40
A NOTE ON PLANNING 43

CHAPTER 4 SCHEDULING SHOOTS 45

MAKING A SHOOTING SCRIPT 50
STORYBOARD 55
ASSEMBLING THE SCHEDULE 56

Loose Ends	57
Chapter 5	61
The Production Process Begins	61

CHAPTER 5 KNOW YOUR LIMITATIONS 61

Delegating	62
Hiring a Line Producer	64
Working with Budgets	66
Going Over Budget	69
Big Concerns for Producers	71

CHAPTER 6 POST-PRODUCTION 79

Getting the Film Finished	79
Modern Editing	82
Starting the Editing	83
Sound	87
Putting Together a Film Score	92
Special Effects	100
When to Cut Effects	108
The Tough Cuts	109
Commercial Viability: It Matters	115

CHAPTER 7 DISTRIBUTION 117

Why Bother?	117
Distribution Models	119
The Traditional Distribution Model	119
Getting Your Materials Ready	123
Understanding What the Distributor Wants, and the Theaters	129
How Long Should a Distribution Deal Last?	133
Domestic and Foreign	134

CHAPTER 8 FILM FESTIVALS AND MARKETS 151

Festivals Overview	151
Film Market Overview	160

CHAPTER 9 163

ADDITIONAL INFORMATION 163

WHEN YOU NEED A LAWYER 164
INTELLECTUAL PROPERTY 168
OWN YOUR FILM: DON'T END UP LIKE *NIGHT OF THE LIVING DEAD* 170

CHAPTER 10 MARKETING IDEAS FOR A DIGITAL AGE ... 175

GETTING THE BUZZ OUT, LITERALLY 175
CONCLUSION 181

PHOTO CREDITS 183

Intro

The producer is the one who makes a film happen. Producers are at the top of the chain of command and are responsible for everything below them. They deal with questions of artistry and money, actors and crew, marketing and distribution. They make sure that those who contributed to the film benefit from its success but, unfortunately, take much of the blame when a film is a failure.

Being a producer is not for the faint of heart; it is for those who know the film industry inside and out and who are driven to be a part of it at every level. It is for the person who knows the difference between different formats, different techniques and even different cameras, and who also knows how contracts are written and secured.

The producer is oftentimes the brains and the brawn that makes a film possible. They are always the one with the most responsibility for a production and, even though they often don't get as much credit as the actors or directors on a film, they have more to do with making that film a reality than most people understand. There's nothing more gratifying in the world for people who are gifted at production than making an idea into a film and, sometimes, even making it into a legend.

Chapter 1

The Scope of Producing a Film

The work of a film producer involves long hours, tough budgets, coordinating many people and, if it's done right, making a great end product.

Successfully producing a film requires managing sometimes very contentious relationships between the talent and crew involved in the production of the film. It requires finding funding, managing it honestly and effectively and, sometimes, getting more to finish a project when things go over budget.

Filmmaking is a dynamic process, one that is always subject to changes and surprises but that must also be done according to a solid, executable plan. Coordinating cash, resources, human beings and the rest of what goes into making a film is no easy undertaking. When it results in a great film it's always worthwhile.

For a Moment, Be Practical

This book is targeted at people looking to produce a film with a budget between $400,000 and $5,000,000, not micro-budget films or backyard zombie adventures shot on digital with a cast of anyone the director knows. These are serious films.

The first thing required is money. It's romantic to say that a great script or a great vision for a film are the starting points, but creativity won't pay for a single frame of film. Until there are finances, there is no way to pay the people required to make the film, to market the film, or to release the film as widely as possible.

To get an idea of what you'll be dealing with, here is an outline of how film budgets are spent.

If you're going to produce a film, you need physical space to handle basic office duties. Major studios usually dedicate around 10% of their budget to this.

You'll need to pay the big-ticket people hired onto the film. These include the writer, the director, the cast and the producer of the film. The costs are usually negotiated before the movie is budgeted. You'll have to figure out how much the director, producer and other leaders in the filmmaking process will be compensated. Getting good people to fill these roles costs money.

Your crew will have to be paid , and this may be an area of the budget where you can reduce costs by being creative. , people at local film schools may be willing to intern on films and this could bring down your expenses.

You'll still need experienced people and this will require that you pay them fairly. Most professionals are members of unions, that publish a minimum pay scale.

When the film is finished, you're going to need distribution. Distributors vary widely in what they charge, with larger, powerful distributors demanding more for their services. Some independent films manage to get noticed, and distributed, after being shown at film festivals.

Part of your budget will depend upon how widely the film will be distributed. If you want to get it seen all over the nation, that's going to cost more money but there is greater potential for returns.

Can It Even Be Done?

When looking at the above breakdown, keep in mind that it doesn't even include miscellaneous costs, such as having video processed and formatted. It also doesn't include costs such as special effects, transportation and other expenses that will be required for the film.

Is it even possible to make a good film on a low budget?

Yes, it is. Some films have been remarkably successful, even though they had very low budgets. Consider the following films and how much they made:

- The Blair Witch Project:
- Budget: $60,000
- Gross: $140,539,000 USA
- Napoleon Dynamite
- Budget: $400,000
- Gross: $44,540, 956 USA
- Halloween (1978):
- Budget: $325, 000
- Gross $60,000,000 Worldwide

*All figures from IMDB.com

Note that the budget for each of these films is at the bottom of or even below the lowest budget addressed in this book. These are all well-known, very popular films that, in two out of three cases, launched franchises. Halloween, , launched one of the largest horror franchises in history.

It is possible to make a great film for $400,000, and for less. It's certainly possible to make a great film for $5,000,000, but that budget *will* get spent and, to some considerable extent, the budget you have to work with will dictate the concept of the film. Details—

i.e., do the astronauts go into space on screen or does that take place off-screen?

Finding the right people has a significant bearing on the scope of putting together an independent film.

Great Script, Awful Acting, Horrible Camera Operator

It is not hard to find examples of independent films that try hard, but fail due to the shortcomings of how they were put together or the people involved.

It's necessary to have professionals, even if the production cannot afford top-of-the-line talent. You're not going to be able to get Kevin Spacey on the budget that most independent films have but, then again, there are talented actors who haven't yet made a name for themselves and are looking for an opportunity. Camera operators, directors of photography, and other important people in the production of the film need to be as high a quality as the budget allows.

Watch some independent films and you'll see hallmarks of people who are in over their heads. For example, bad script development oftentimes results in:

- Scenes that go nowhere, and do it for several minutes
- Plot lines that are introduced and dropped for no reason either way
- Characters that mysteriously appear and disappear
- Continuity errors
- Unrealistic dialog
- Clichés
- Pastiches of other films

Films that have directors that are a bit more talented and experienced in theory than in reality oftentimes have:

- Continuity errors
- Poorly-composed shots and sequences
- Shots that go on for far too long
- Boring composition—no transitions between wide shots and close-ups during dialogue
- Lots of unnecessary shots

Using these two key creators as an example, consider what their opposites tend to do. Good screenwriters keep films moving forward all the time. Dialogue always advances the plot. Characters are sensible in the sense of how they behave to what goes on in the story. Lines that say nothing are clipped out of the screenplay altogether. That kind of talent costs money.

Good directors make people forget that they're watching a movie. They don't see special effects shortcomings because they want the action to be real. The characters become people the audience feels like they know, because they are shot in interesting and skillful ways. The film has a clear three or four acts and the audience doesn't feel ripped off at the end.

No matter how good the director, director of photography, set designers and other crew are, they cannot rescue a script that isn't up to par. A great script in the hands of an incompetent director is wasted. Pay for the talent: it's an investment and returns are relative to the amount invested.

Sometimes the lack of a talented team is in the spirit of maintaining an independent film "voice." This is a huge mistake.

Don't Sacrifice Your Film to Silly Ideals

The biggest mistake that independent filmmakers make, according to many people's own experience, is to be uncompromising. Some independent filmmakers fancy themselves the next Tarantino, whose visions are too out there for the studios to understand, and who must take total control of the film. Screenwriters, for example, may feel like their product is the result of a flash of genius that will redefine the film world provided it isn't watered down by producers and other craven types only concerned with the bottom line. This can end up making it difficult to get the rights to a script without having to heed the demands of a good writer who is, unfortunately, a horrible filmmaker.

To produce a film, you're going to need some flexibility in the people you work with and yourself. Your idea will be changed based on the demands and better ideas that come from funders, studios, directors, writers, and so forth.

This is the way the film business works. While major directors, producers, and stars get a lot of credit and glory for films—and a huge chunk of the budget—they need other people to help them through the process. The people who direct talent and resources need talent and resources to direct, and they have to sometimes compromise to make a film better.

You'll want *"no"* people rather than *"yes"* people involved in the film. You'll need people who will tell you:

- *When the basic idea needs a lot of work;*
- *When the idea may be too derivative of other films;*
- *When the people you want to hire aren't up to standards;*
- *When you have to do the very hard stuff, such as letting people go because they're not measuring up.*

Remember that many film producers come from other parts of the film industry, in which they may have extensive experience. This doesn't mean that first-time producers are at a natural disadvantage, but it does mean that there is a learning curve involved. Writers will usually know a lot about optioning rights and getting ideas developed that help them in their roles as producers. Directors understand the nuts and bolts of how an idea makes it onto a film. Experience in any area of filmmaking is desirable in a producer, but not necessary. If you surround yourself with honest, qualified people, you can take advantage of what they know to make the right decisions for the project.

Love Your Work

As we progress through the chapters, you will find that there's a lot involved in being a producer that you may not have thought about. Even if you've done it before, there are resources and information in the following chapters that will help future endeavors. The most important asset you need is a love for the filmmaking process.

As a producer, you will be involved in every step of the filmmaking process. You'll be a part of it all, from finding out the concept to developing scripts that make that concept into a workable story. You'll find talent for the film and participate in every aspect of what happens once the film starts being shot and long after.

The rewards can be tremendous. This is one of the most desirable and sought-after positions in the filmmaking industry. Producers are responsible for some of the decisions that make the best films in the world worth watching over and over again. They're also responsible for some real blunders. Some of them get very, very rich and enjoy the freedom to produce most anything they want.

Filmmaking is a tough business, but if you love the challenge and the form, then you might end up with the film you've always dreamed of producing and enjoy further success down the line.

References

http://gideonsway.wordpress.com/2012/05/06/film-money/

http://indiemoviemaking.com/the-single-biggest-mistake-a-filmmaker-can-make/ - more-892

Chapter 2

The Work of Production

Producing a film is a demanding and intricate process. It has many different phases. It starts with getting the rights to a story that you want to produce as a film. There are various ways to go about this, but, to get a good story, the writer will have to be compensated somehow. There are those rare types that manage to write and produce a movie and, if you're one of them, you simply have to lock down your rights to the story so that you get paid for the work you did.

Getting the Rights

The first step in getting the rights is to determine whether or not someone else already has the film rights, even where smaller, lesser-known stories are concerned. There are situations where the rights are available, but the current owner of those rights may not want to sell them to you. There are also cases where someone won't want to sell the rights to film their work to anyone, fearing that they'd lose creative control, allowing the process of adaptation to ruin the story. There are other stations that you may run into.

Who Can You Get Rights From?

You don't need to get the rights to a well-known, popular story to make a great film. The film *It's a Wonderful Life*, one of the best-known films in the world, was optioned from a story that was never even published. There are many places you can look and, if you're looking to get the rights to a story with a lot of potential, consider the following sources:

- *Short stories, published or unpublished*
- *Magazine articles*
- *Outlined, but not fully-written, stories*
- *Public domain sources—more on this below*
- *Non-fiction works*

Anywhere you find a good story that you think could be a great film, you have an opportunity. The key element is making sure that you recognize those opportunities and don't overlook them. When you do find a story you want to work with, you may run into any of the following situations.

The Rights Aren't Available and the Author Doesn't Want to Give Them Up

So, you've found a great book that you know would make a great film. It has all the trappings of a great low-budget film. It doesn't demand advanced FX, the story is tight and compelling, and filming it would fit within your budget, but the author doesn't want to sell the film rights.

In these situations, you're best off moving along and finding something else. You could spend all of your time negotiating with a reluctant author or you could find another story. Keep the following in mind.

There are very few original stories out there. Most of them fit within genres—action, thriller, fantasy, horror, etc.—and there are plenty of authors writing those stories. You always have options.

The Preproduction Process

Some authors genuinely do not want their material filmed and you'll waste a lot of time trying to persuade them otherwise. If they're not interested, find someone who is.

Sometimes, the person or entity that owns the rights may be persuadable. This is where your people skills come into play. You might be able to get them to relent and to sell you the film rights. It may be a matter of who's attached to the project, . If the director is Sam Nobody and he has no work to speak of, the rights owner may not want him to handle the directing. If the director is a well-known name, they may reconsider, anticipating good results.

Be aware that some authors will try to milk every last penny they can out of their options. This may be because they don't understand the ballpark range for film options, particularly if you're working with an author who does have an agent.

Sources such as Writer's Digest place the figure that authors should expect at a floor of $500 and up to $5,000, if they have something good. If you're determined to get the rights to film a particular story and the owner is asking for too much, explain to them how they'll get compensated once the story starts filming. The option is only the initial amount of money that they'll make. They stand to make a lot more if there's a substantial budget for the film with an agreement to share in any potential profits.

TIP: Arguing that exposure is a great reason for a reluctant author to sell the option for their film may or may not work. Some authors will desire to write for film and will jump at this. Others won't care, but it can be persuasive to sell options and reinforce that, if the film gets made, the author may get a lot of recognition and more work.

The Current Owner of the Rights Want to Sell

If the author wants to sell, you'll have to figure out what it's worth to you to get the story you have in mind.

You may want someone to help you work through the negotiation process. If the author has an agent, this should be pretty straightforward, as the agent will likely have experience on that front.

If you can option the story you're interested in, consider the following:

Who will be interested in this story? If you're buying something that neatly fits into a genre, this should be obvious. Horror movies have a built-in audience, as do fantasy movies. If the story is less clear in terms of where it fits, make sure that you're buying something that's going to Find an audience.

Make sure that the story isn't too derivative of other films on the market or you're at risk of producing something that is only an alternate version of a story that viewers can get somewhere else or a bad pastiche of a film that's already been made.

There is something to be said for getting in on a craze and for genres that always sell. After *Lord of the Rings* had its run, there was still plenty of appetite for films and television series in a similar vein. The release of *Hostel* didn't quash audience appetites for films such as *Saw*, even though they are the same type of horror.

Consider whether the film that could be made from the story would be original enough to stand out on its own merits. If not, there may be better options out there, even within the same basic genre.

Working from a Pitch

You may at some point run into an author who has a great idea, but not a finished product. This can get tricky. They may want to get paid—they almost certainly want to get paid, —if that idea is made into a film.

This is a sketchy area because, if you have a screenwriter put together a script using that author's ideas, you could end up in some trouble.

Copyright is difficult to understand. Consider the information below if you plant to take the basic premise of a pitch and develop it.

The Preproduction Process

> *"Copyright is a protection that covers published and unpublished literary, scientific, and artistic works, whatever the form of expression, provided such works are fixed in a tangible or material form. This means that if you can see it, hear it and/or touch it – it may be protected."*

If you're in doubt, consult with a lawyer about the matter. Listen to your own sense of ethics in this regard. If it seems like you're stealing someone else's idea and shutting them out of the potential profits, you probably are.

What the Owner Will Expect

You absolutely must have a contract in place before you proceed to make a film out of someone else's original work. The negotiation process can be brutal.

The author will likely want a fee for selling you the rights, somewhere between $500 and $5,000, as given above. The author will also likely want a percentage fee based on the total cost of production for the film, plus a percentage of the box office take and a percentage of sales in other formats, including DVDs and online streaming.

Most producers will want to reduce these payments or eliminate them altogether. Whether or not the writer agrees depends upon whether there has been interest expressed in their film and, directly, how much they need the cash.

Expect the negotiations to take some time and don't expect to get the option for a great story for a ridiculous offer. Make sure that the writer isn't taking you for a ride, however. All contracts have to be examined by a lawyer.

Once you get the option, you'll have a given amount of time, usually one year, to make the film. After this, you'll have to negotiate again. When you're ready to get the option on a story, be ready to start production so that you satisfy this requirement.

Films that get optioned, but never get made are oftentimes described as being in *"development hell."* This means that someone has the option but, for whatever reason, the film doesn't get made. You don't want to end up here, and neither does the creator of the property.

Buying a Script

In some cases, you'll run across a writer who has a developed script. This can be great for cutting costs. Aside from doctoring and improving it, you'll only have to turn it into a shooting script.

Make sure you get the author to agree to let your writers revise the script. You'll likely have to make alterations and you don't want an inexperienced writer having enough control to prevent you from making sensible changes.

Writing a Script

There are professional screenwriters who are always writing. One of your options is to work with one of them.

This allows you to get a script made to your specifications. It also allows you to have a lot more control over the story from the start, which could cut down on the revisions.

The biggest advantage of going this route is dealing with someone who is experienced with writing scripts and with the business that surrounds it. They're less likely to make ridiculous demands regarding control or compensation.

You can use any of the resources available to all filmmakers to find a writer for your project. Consider contacting the following agencies or using the following advertising venues to seek writers:

- *The Writers Guild of America*
- *Script Magazine*
- *Hollywood Reporter*
- *Creative Screenwriting*
- *Writer's Digest*

You may also use your existing network of the people already attached to the film. The director may know screenwriters who will do a good job. This can be a real advantage for a producer, as it eliminates the wildcard of getting options for a story and turning it into a script. Starting with a script written by a pro can be a huge advantage.

If you have the skills, you can go the George Lucas route and write, produce, and direct the entire project. However, this will to be a hard sell to anyone putting up the funding.

Books Into a Script

Many great films are the results of taking a book and adapting it for the screen. Some of the most successful franchises started out this way,

including the aforementioned *Lord of the Rings* and *Game of Thrones*. For a low-budget film, there are good options out there. You're obviously not going to be able to produce a continent-sprawling epic fantasy adventure on $400,000 to $5,000,000, but there are options.

Remember that you don't have to start with a full-length book. There are great short stories that could easily be made into films. Consider the following venues for finding books, short or long, that you could turn into a script.

- *Amazon: see what eBooks are selling well.*
- *Short fiction magazines: Apex and Analogue are both examples of magazines that publish short stories.*
- *Non-fiction: Sometimes someone's personal story makes for a compelling film, and the option may be very affordable.*

You will need the author to allow you to have your own scriptwriters turn the book into a script. Some authors will be more than happy about this, as it basically allows them to get in on the profits for a film version of their work without having to do the work of writing a script themselves, which not all authors particularly want to do.

The Public Domain

The public domain is a goldmine for producers. These are works of art that aren't owned by anyone. There are various reasons why this happens:

- *The ownership of the property has expired, usually due to it being very old;*
- *The property was never properly copyrighted;*
- *The property was offered into the public domain by the creator.*

The Preproduction Process

Within the public domain, consider that some of the following works are available and that no one has the rights to them. That means, , that you can make them into a script without asking anyone's permission and do so however you choose:

Here are some of the books that are in the public domain:

- *Dracula by Bram Stoker;*
- *The Picture of Dorian Grey by Oscar Wilde;*
- *Anne of Green Gables by L.M. Montgomery;*
- *The Wonderful Wizard of Oz by L. Frank Baum;*
- *The Metamorphosis by Franz Kafka.*

Some of these films, such as *The Wonderful Wizard of Oz*, have already been used as source material for successful—even legendary—adaptations. Any public domain work can be freely used and adapted, so consider these fair game. Make sure you have a complete search for rights to any property done before you do adapt it, however. Consider the following:

H.P. Lovecraft is one of the best-known American horror writers. Much of his work predates 1923, which means that it is in the public domain, according to one argument. Much of Lovecraft's work was published much later, which means that there is disagreement as to whether or not his works—or, at least, some of them—are in the public domain right now.

If a lot of people are interested in a particular work that you believe to be in the public domain, be sure you have it researched. There have been changes to the law made in the 1970s and 2000s that extended the length of copyrights. It's also unclear, in some cases, whether or not the copyright was renewed and you may have to dig into this to determine whether a work is in the public domain. Remember: controversy means that there is a potential for a lawsuit if you make something that someone else claims to own the rights to. There are also differences in copyright law around the world, so it's always a good idea to do your research, even if you have every reason to believe that a piece of work is in the public domain.

Tips for Dealing with Property Owners

If your efforts are being foiled by a property owner that won't sell, consider the following things that might persuade them to be more open-minded.

-You're offering something: Having a book or short story optioned is a tremendous opportunity for any author.

-Many books are published with the options offered. It's not uncommon for the rights to new novels to be immediately available.

-There's plenty out there. If you can't get someone to relinquish the option, go elsewhere.

-Consider dealing with a publishing house or an agent rather than dealing with individual authors.

-Look at independent publishers. They're oftentimes very eager to sell material to the right buyer and may be more accommodating where price is concerned.

-Remember that the advent of eBooks and self-publishing have hit big publishing houses hard. Don't discount them, as they may have properties that they are very eager to option into films.

Chapter 3

The Preproduction Process

Producers put in some of their longest days at the job before the film is shot. Some of the tasks involved are major, such as getting the director and the other people involved with the film signed on. Others may seem minor but, if they aren't handled correctly, the entire production could fall apart or turn out to be more expensive and difficult to complete.

The following information will help you to understand how some of the most significant tasks involved in the preproduction process get done and help you understand why some details are vital to the success of a film production.

Fixing the Script

Scriptwriters have a great deal of information available to them about what they need to produce as a spec script. A spec script is the script a screenwriter presents when they are trying to sell it. Unfortunately, as many sites and books for screenwriters point out, screenwriters tend to produce a sort of halfway-to-shooting script and the script will likely need work before it's ready to shoot, of.

Making a Real Spec Script

A shooting script is only produced after the spec script has been purchased. Many sources that give advice to up-and-coming screenwriters point out that screenwriters tend to put a lot of directions in their scripts, essentially making spec scripts sort of shooting scripts. These same sources advise writers not to do this, but writers persist, anyway. Most of the time, the suggestions aren't worth keeping, though there may be a few instances where there are some good ideas that can be built upon.

The useful items will be the most general, such as Interior – Hotel Room – Day. The things you can cut include:

- *Calls for specific shots;*
- *Music cues;*
- *Direction for how special effects should be done.*

What you want from the script is a great story. The members of your crew, and you, will have the specific skills to translate that story into a film.

When you have your script all ready to go, it will be very simple. You'll have the narrative of the action that will be taking place on screen, along with the character's lines. This doesn't have to be sophisticated and marked up with technical information. It should be neither of those things. The spec script should make it easy to follow the story and you'll use it to pitch the idea to directors and other crewmembers, in many cases, so it should be an easy read.

The quality of the spec script you end up with should be high enough to persuade a good director, good actors, and a good crew to sign on.

Time: How Long Will the Film Be?

Most of the time, filmmakers equate one page of script with one minute of film time. If you want a 90-minute film, therefore, the script should be roughly 90 pages. If, someone asks you how long the film you're producing will be, giving them an estimate based on this convention is entirely acceptable. It's accurate enough.

Finding the Director

The job of film director is not so easily described. There are several factors that go into determining the director's responsibilities, including their experience and reputation.

In the chain of command, the director is second only to the producer, and sometimes equal to the producer. Their position affects how much authority they have over the film's creative process. The right director will be able to pick up slack where the producer is weak and will be able to stand back and take direction when the producer needs something to be taken care of in a certain way. In order to understand which director is right for any given film, it's useful to put them into a few different categories.

The Director for Hire

All directors are for hire , but in this case the term refers to those directors who could be described as workmanlike. They don't have much creative control over the film and may be putting together their shots based on what the producer told them.

These types of directors are usually not as experienced. The advantage with this type of director is that, as a producer, you naturally will have more creative control without input.

The More Experienced Director

This would be a director who has done a lot of work in the industry and who has a good reputation, but who isn't a celebrity. Think of this type of director as the kind that you can instruct but don't have to micromanage. They know the conventions for shooting action, horror, comedy, and so forth, are good at what they do, and have a solid reputation. These types of directors are excellent if you want a more hands-off approach, but want to make sure that you're ultimately in charge of the film and don't have to worry about your every decision being challenged or argued against.

The Celebrity Director
If your budget is in the $400,000 to $5,000,000 range, this director is probably out of reach. There may be exceptions, however.

Spielberg, Stone, Cameron and other directors are at this level. If you attach one of these directors to your film, you can be nearly certain that you'll get great results. You can also be nearly certain that this type of director will demand complete creative control of the film.

These directors can be great for marketing a film and, sometimes, their names will get people into the theater more than will the actual stars or story. These directors may make the producer feel like the second person in the chain of command and that may not be tenable.

Qualifications
There are directors out there who are very successful and who have no college degree. Quentin Tarantino is an example of such a director. Most successful directors have degrees. Keep in mind that a director has to have a lot more than a creative vision. They have to know how to use every tool at their disposal—sound, lights, staging, sets, framing shots, etc.---to create a great film. Without a degree, you have no guarantee that a director knows a gel from a lens filter and, while they may be creative and good at directing people, they may ultimately have no idea what they're doing.

If you're making a serious film, start out by looking for people who have the education to back up what they claim to be able to do for the project. If they don't, be skeptical.

Body of Work

One of the best ways to find a director is to look at what directors that might be interested in your project have produced in the past. This should give you an idea of their style and skill level and can help to determine if they'd be a good match for your project.

Directors are always on the hunt for projects that they can add to their resumes. Those directors who are serious will likely have something to show for their efforts and, on top of a degree, they'll have completed projects. Review the director's reel to determine whether that director is right for your project.

Networks

A good way to start is by exploiting your own network. People you know may be aware of someone looking for a project. Everyone knows that the film business is largely about personal networks and, when you're producing, take advantage of them to find the right people, if possible.

Unions

Established directors may belong to the Director's Guild of America (DGA). These directors will come with a minimum requirement for their weekly salary, as well as minimum lengths of employment and other union required conditions.

If you want to work with a union crew, you'll need to work with a union director. The advantage is that the union isn't open to anyone and everyone and the members are all legitimate practitioners of their trade.

How Directors Are Paid

To attach to a film, directors will usually require that they have a salary and that you guarantee them that they'll be employed for a certain amount of time. Their time of employment may encompass the preproduction phase, production, and the postproduction phase, so you'll need to be clear about those terms before deciding on a given director.

The director will also want some amount of money for signing onto the project. Remember that the project can still fall through, and the director has to make sure that the time they spend waiting to find out isn't a complete waste for them. You can negotiate sign-up bonuses or you can offer a percentage of the total budget. You can also offer incentives, such as a percentage of the box office take. Some directors may be amicable to taking less money if they're given more control over the project, which is s an option if the director is out of your budget otherwise.

The Name Counts
You may end up fund raising after you have gotten a director and a good script. The funding can be easier to get if you attach a director with a good reputation for making profitable film. Then again, if you have a very talented unknown with some impressive work to show, you may find investors are very interested in helping to foster that talent.

The bottom line is that, if you have a good script and a good director, you have an advantage in securing funding.

Hiring the Cast
Finding good directors can be tough, because in spite of their ability, not all directors will be right for your project. Where actors are concerned, it's also tough, but for different reasons.

There's no requirement that you have to meet to call yourself an actor. It's not like being a doctor, where you have to have the appropriate licenses to practice. This means that finding the right cast will be a filtering process more than anything. For the type of money that low-budget films can offer, big names are usually out of the question. The word *usually* is important there. Actors are artists and, if you have a great script and a great director, a big name may take a personal interest in the project.

Since that is an unlikely scenario, prepare for the grind of finding actors on your own.

Consider a Casting Director

A casting director can be an enormous asset for a producer. These are people that take all the information about the actors who express an interest in a film and sort through it, looking for the best of the best. If the casting director likes an actor's resume and qualifications, they'll pass them along to you.

Remember: You're still in charge. Your casting director makes sure that your time isn't being wasted, but they don't make decisions about who gets hired and who does not. You do.

If you have a casting director, be aware that you'll vastly expand your network of available actors. The casting director can probably think of a few people who will fit any given role. They will also likely be familiar with actors who are looking for work, and that means that you might be able to get a very good actor at a lower price than you would pay for someone with a more established name and reputation.

Remember that this isn't ripping off an actor by paying them less than they're worth. Many up-and-coming actors, if they see a great script, are right for the role, and get along with the producer and director, will be very enthusiastic about throwing themselves into a role. It's a big opportunity. The $400,000 to $5,000,000 budget may not avail you of huge names, but it certainly gives you enough to make the job interesting for actors who are looking to become the next big name.

Agents and Agencies

You can also look for actors with help from an agency or an individual agent. There's something about this business that actors and producers both need to understand.

Reputable agents and agencies don't charge actors up-front fees for their services. The actors get charged when the agent gets them a gig and the fee is usually a percentage of what the actor is getting paid for the project. Most of the time, this will be somewhere around 10%. As the producer, understand this when budgeting for actors.

Some agencies will want you to pay the percentage fee on top of what you're paying the actor. This means that, whatever price you negotiated for the actor, it went up 10%. This is usually not a deal breaker for anyone, but keep it in mind when working with agencies. If you're not amicable to covering the agent's costs, you might want to use this as a point that you can negotiate.

Some actors may be willing to work for less if they get a percentage of DVD sales, box office receipts. and so forth. Be cautious in this regard, as giving actors a percentage of the film's receipts can become a burden for the studio or other agency funding the film. A percentage of the box-office receipts means that, even if the film loses money, the actor gets paid.

Remember that receipts don't equal profit.

Advertising

Actors are always looking for work. One way to find them is submitting an advertisement seeking actors. These are commonly seen in newspapers, magazines, and on websites.

The advertisements should be very specific. Because the characters in a film will all have a certain look, the advertisement needs to specify this. Otherwise, you might get a bunch of 120-pound smokers auditioning for the role of a boxer.

Advertising is a great way to get extras for a film. The descriptions still matter. , if you were shooting a film that had a scene in a dive bar, the advertisement might read:

"Extras Needed for Film Project: Male and female, all body types, able to pull off a tough look preferred."

This will ensure that you get the people with a few scars here and there, tough faces and intimidating bodies rather than unblemished actors who would be more at home as extras in a suburban mall scene.

Friend Networks

It's a very bad idea to hire an actor because they are a friend. It's also a bad idea to hire an actor because you want to cement your reputation with someone who has more pull in the filmmaking scene than you.

When you hire an actor, hire them because they fit the role and because they have the kind of work ethic that defines a professional. Prima donnas will suck up your budget, waste your time, and be very demanding.

What to Ask For

When you're looking at actors for a role, there's a standard package that expect. It should contain a headshot of the actor, their resume, and their agency's contact information or the actor's direct contact information, if they don't have an agency.

One of the advantages of having a casting director is that any actor information that doesn't contain that listed above will be tossed, saving you the time of looking at resumes from people who clearly aren't professional-level actors.

A Novel Way to Find Extras
Finding the leads for a film may be pretty easy, given that you'll be the one doing the picking and choosing. There are plenty of actors to choose from out there and most of them are looking for work.

With extras, you might want to save some money and, instead of asking them to come to you, go to them. If you need extras for a skateboard movie, go to the local skate park. If you need extras to play bikers, go to a bike rally. It's a good way to find people and, because you'll see them in person right away, you'll be able to tell if they're the right type of extra for the job.

Hiring the Crew

There are many people who contribute to the making of any film, but there are some types of workers that are entirely indispensable. Your budget and the scope of the project will determine which types of crewmembers you need. The following are likely to be ones that you cannot do without.

Script Supervisor
Every movie starts with a compelling story and a script supervisor makes sure that the details of the story are represented accurately. They handle a lot of different types of work, from making sure that scenes are set up properly to ensuring that continuity errors don't make it into the film.

The script supervisor has to be fastidious, efficient and never miss a detail. They have to make sure that the film that has burning candles in one scene doesn't show them as having gotten longer in another scene that takes place after the first. They have to make sure that the actors are consistent in terms of their appearance. An actor with a black eye from a fight scene needs to have the same black eye in every scene that follows and the script supervisor makes sure that it happens.

The script supervisor may also keep track of technical details. They may be the one member of the crew who wrote down which type of microphone was used in a given scene, so that the audio is consistent. They may even go through the script and compare what was called for in a scene to what was shot and point out if something was missing.

The script supervisor also makes sure that some of the more embarrassing errors that sometimes plague low-budget films don't happen. If an actor suddenly changes the way they're using their accent and starts pronouncing a word differently, the script supervisor may well be the one to point out that there's a problem.

You'll want someone good in this role, and you'll want someone who is utterly uncompromising in terms of pointing out details that are getting missed.

If you want to see the results of poor script supervision, it's not hard to find, unfortunately. Palm trees in Illinois were one of the big problems with attention to detail in the film *Halloween*.

After the shooting is done, the notes that the script supervisor took will be indispensable, so be sure you hire someone with experience who is an expert record keeper and who knows film. Someone with a working knowledge of cameras and lenses is also desirable, as the script supervisor may keep track of them for the director so that shots are consistent.

Assistant Director

The assistant director helps the director to do their job. They don't do any direction themselves.

The assistant director, if you want another example of a chain of command with clear roles, is the sergeant if the director is an officer. The assistant director finds out what the director needs and makes sure that the director has it. The assistant director finds out what the director wants the cast to do and makes sure that they do it.

The assistant director needs to be someone that the director can work with and someone that you, as the producer, can work with. Remember that the assistant director also needs to be someone who doesn't mind being unpopular. The director is not likely to hear every complaint that the cast and crew, have but the assistant director will.

Some directors will have an assistant that they want to work with. This is a good thing for the film, as it means there is a readymade team between the director and the assistant director.

Director of Photography
This role is oftentimes referred to as the DP. Technically, in terms of their skill set, they are cinematographers. They have more to do with making great films than most people might think. On a large-budget film, the DP usually doesn't handle the actual operation of the camera, though they may. On low-budget films, it's more likely that the DP will also do the cinematography directly.

When the director has a great idea for a shot, the DP makes it happen. When you see a great close-up, cutaway or any other type of shot in a film, the DP had nearly as much to do with it as the director.

Some directors will get behind the camera once in a while, but their skills are broader and need to be distributed between many different tasks. The DP is only concerned with getting every shot perfect. If you get a good DP, you will be get those types of shots. Here's what to look for:

- *Experience working in the film's format: i.e. digital and film;*

The Preproduction Process

- *Experience working across genres and styles;*
- *Education: Good self-taught cinematographers are rare;*
- *A relationship with the director: Some directors will insist on a certain DP. Get them, if you can.*

Sound

Unless you are shooting a silent film, sound will be as important to your film as the visuals. You'll need a good sound team. There are sound mixers, people who hold the mics— called boom people— and many others involved in getting the sound together for a film. You need excellent technicians in each of those jobs.

The bonus here is that these services usually come as a package deal.

Remember that sound is not finished when shooting ends. You'll also need access to studio time for sound production. The people who handle this type of work need to be qualified and to have the right equipment for the job.

Lights

You absolutely must have someone qualified to work with dangerous electrical equipment for the lighting on any movie set. This person is known as the gaffer. They set up the lighting, which is a big job in and of itself, and also ensure that everything is wired together correctly so that there is no damage or injury. There needs to be a certified electrician with film experience on the set. Without them, you cannot ensure safety, and that's a huge problem for any film. The electrician also makes sure that you don't misuse and damage expensive equipment.

Your gaffer and best boy should have resumes and they may well come as a team. They handle a lot of responsibility at the shoot.

Makeup

Good makeup artists handle character appearance details. Some may work with prosthetics for aging, simulating wounds, or transforming a character into a non-human creature.

Makeup artists are very easy to screen. Look at their resume and at photographs or videos of the work that they've done on other films.

Wardrobe

The big boss here is the wardrobe designer. They'll come up with the looks for the characters, along with the producer, the director.

There are tricks that an experienced wardrobe department worker can use to cut production costs. They get characters ready for a scene that requires different wardrobe in the same setting. The also attend to continuity. On smaller productions, wardrobe needs may be much less involved, but they're still important. Look for someone creative for this role. If you want an illustration of how important wardrobe can be for a character, consider how Luke Skywalker's wardrobe demonstrates the evolution of his character throughout the first three movies in that series. He goes from a simple farm boy in white peasant clothing to an ace fighter pilot wearing a flight suit to a Jedi knight wearing an entirely black priest/warrior ensemble.

Laborers

Every film needs laborers to handle the heavy lifting, running cables handling equipment, and myriad other tasks. The people you may need include:

- *Painters;*
- *Plumbers;*
- *General laborers;*
- *Carpenters.*

There could be more, depending upon your set. These people are directly overseen by the construction manager, who should be someone with a lot of experience not only in film, but in contracting.

For a low-budget film, you may not need a full complement of laborers, particularly if the sets are simple..

Your set designers should be able to identify the skilled labor required to produce the set. This can be hashed out during the breakdown process, where locations are identified.

Swing Gang

No matter how organized and well planned your shoot is, there is a probability of last minute changes This is where the swing gang comes into play. If the door on the closet needs to be removed—*now*—the swing gang will handle it. The swing gang is invaluable. They provide a resource that keeps the production moving when something isn't right about the set. Make sure that you have people to handle this important position.

Art Department

The art department contains a variety of different people, but they all concentrate on getting the right look for a film. The art director works with the higher-ups, including the director, to make the director's vision for the film a reality.

Within the art department, you'll find everyone from the set decorators to the storyboard illustrators to the swing gang.

On a low-budget production, you may have to get by with a smaller art department, but a good art director can make a film stand out. While the director may have a vision, and while you may have one yourself, it's the art department that's going to realize that vision, so look for good people to fill this role.

Music

As a producer, a lot of your job will be pouring through resumes, making tough decisions, and hoping you hire the right people. Finding the right person to make the music for your film can be a refreshing break. Essentially, you spend this part of the production process listening to music and deciding on which composer is right for your film.

Most of the time, films are scored by a classically trained composer using a full or partial orchestra. This isn't your only option. Using electronics, you can skip the orchestra and cut down on costs. A composer who uses these types of instruments can be a huge asset as far as your budget is concerned.

Remember not to underestimate the power of music to make a film successful. Even some films that have been flops—*Purple Rain, Dune*—are still notable for their soundtracks and those soundtracks continue to sell.

As alternatives to traditional film composers, consider the following options:

- *Electronic composers;*
- *Up-and-coming bands;*

- Completely unknown bands. They'll jump at the chance;
- Abstract music composers.

There's no limit here. Listen to some samples of a composer's or band's work and, when you hear something that is perfect for your film, you'll know that you've found a good candidate.

Editors

Deciding upon the right editor is one of the biggest decisions you'll make in terms of how the final product will come out. You'll want someone who is experienced in the format you're using, . If you need someone who can edit physical film, you'll likely have a tougher search ahead of you. Digital editing digital is a skill competently taught at technical schools. Qualifications aren't the most important things, however.

Take a look at their body of work. Like every other creative person involved in filmmaking, editors will have a style that is uniquely their own. This should mesh with what the director and producer expect.

Look for someone who produces a scene that wastes no time, that involves the audience with skillful intercutting of shots, and that transitions seamlessly to the next scene. If you can find an editor who can pull this off, have someone who is well qualified to handle the work you have in front of them.

Package Deals

Producers don't necessarily have to find all of these people—and the others—involved in making a film one-by-one. There are companies that provide a readymade crew—or, at least, a good portion of one—as their business.

You can find them at sites such as:

- *Production Hub;*
- *Film and TV Pro;*
- *Entertainment Careers.*

It is also a good option for finding qualified people. If there's one thing you can do to cut down on the amount of time involved in assembling the crew for a production, it's use the Internet as much as possible. There are job seekers all over these boards and some of them are very well qualified to work on a professional production and have plenty of experience doing so.

Whether you're hiring your crew one-by-one contracting existing production companies with all the help you need available, your film is not ready to start production until you have the right crew. In order to keep the crew working smoothly and up to the level you expect, you'll have to set some standards for them to follow.

Setting Standards

Every single person on your crew has to be top-notch. When you send a location scout and a grip out to check out a potential shooting location, they have to be able to come back with all the information the director needs, including any special problems the location might present. This requires experience and dedication. If you cannot find costume rentals, you better have an art department with at least one qualified tailor or seamstress.

Set standards for everyone on your crew and be sure that they meet them. If you do this right from the start, you won't have to deal with firing and rehiring for positions on your production. If you don't expect high standards from your crew, you'll get a substandard film, every time. Here are some things that insist upon:

- *All crewmembers show up on time at shoots;*

- *Crewmembers anticipate staying late if necessary, and they get compensated well for doing so;*
- *All crewmembers should be professional, courteous and respect the chain of command;*
- *No supervisory crewmembers should be abusive or treat any of their subordinates like servants. Respect should be expected and given at all levels of the production. It's a high-pressure job with a lot of money riding on the results. Some breakdowns on sets have been captured online and gone viral;*
- *Where necessary, crewmembers should keep accurate logs of their time and what they were doing.*

Remember that some people get a bit of authority and lord it over others, ruining a work environment and destroying team cohesion. If your art director abuses the swing gang to the point where they quit the job, you and your budget are the ones that will suffer.

Confidentiality

Confidentiality: Make sure you have the cast and crew sign a confidentiality agreement. Leaks about films and TV shows have become and are a serious problem for the film industry. Along with whatever specific confidentiality requirements you have, the following should always apply:

- *Any on-set pictures need to be cleared with the producer before they are shared online;*
- *Tweeting, Facebook posting and other social networking on-set should be prohibited;.*

- *Scripts should be tightly guarded. Scripts getting leaked is an all-too-common occurrence these days;*
- *If one of your cast or crew gets interviewed by the media, let them know what they can say and what they can't say;*
- *If you have a social media campaign promoting the film, everything should be cleared with the producer before it is posted.*

Coordination

If you've ever heard the expression "herding cats," you have some idea of what producing a film can be like. Your greatest ally in this task is coordinating the process so that as much of it as possible is predictable. Realize the following: A lot of it will be unpredictable. Your organizational skills can afford you an island of sanity in a sea of chaos, but you're going to have to learn to work with that chaos and have a good plan for reining it in when it gets out of hand.

Communication

If you have a professional film crew on board your production, n't have any trouble with people subverting the chain of command. The set decorator will go to the art director if they have a problem and won't start hassling the director. If the AD has a problem, he or she will speak with the director, but likely will not try to go over the director's head and talk to the producer.

It's your job to set up a communication system that allows everyone to have a voice when they have a problem. Production assistants can take care of a lot of the detail work for you. Make sure that the crew is provided with a way to contact them in the event that they have a problem and need assistance. This includes situations like:

- *An illness that prevents them from carrying out their duties;.*
- *Harassment on the set.*

- *Not getting paid;*
- *Not getting overtime for hours to which they're entitled higher pay;*
- *Someone being disruptive on the set.*

As for the physical means of communication on a set, consider getting handheld radios. Cellular phones are too much of a distraction, though the higher-ups on the set may need them.

You can use the Multi-Use Radio Service (MURS) on-set to keep communications going. This is allowable for business use and it's inexpensive to get handsets. Having this sort of communication is the difference between wasting time relaying messages in person and calling someone onto the set via radio. The communications can be made private and they have a limited range.

There are also private radio services available from companies such as Motorola and others. These may be good options if you're particularly worried about security. General Mobile Radio Service (GMRS) is also an option, but it requires a license to operate.

Chain of Command

Make a chain-of-command flow chart and distribute it to the crew and cast when they get the general information about the shoot. This lets them know who to contact for what. It can cut down on confusion. If something needs attention, this is what the crewmember needs to make sure they report the problem to the person responsible.

Making Tough Decisions

Sometimes, you're going to make a decision doesn't pan out. Your art director may turn out to be impossible for the director to work with. The director may be impossible for you to work with.

There's no easy and fast advice for handing these situations. The thing to remember is that you, as the producer, are charged with safeguarding the funds provided by the financiers or the studio, so you have to make sure you do so. If someone or something isn't working, you'll have to figure out a solution that preserves the budget and the integrity of the film.

Bringing It All Together

You have your cast, you have your crew and you have a great script. What's left to be done?

A lot.

Ideally, everything you need for any given shoot should be ready to go and, when the crew deploys at a location, they should only have to set up the equipment, dress the set, and get the shots that they need. Shooting should be a fast, smooth process, but unfortunately, there are plenty of things that can go wrong and eat up your budget. Here are some things that to monitor closely.

Scouting Locations

Location managers are responsible for handling everything related to finding out where and when to shoot. They even have their own guild, giving some idea of how important this job is. If you're producing a low-budget film, you, the director and other people may want to get involved in scouting locations, but realize that this is detailed work.

There is no right or wrong way to look for locations. If you need a historic house, drive around neighborhoods and look for something suitable. Make sure you have plenty of business cards that you can hand out and, as a precaution, take some letters that let homeowners know that you saw their house and are interested in checking it out as a shooting location. Include your contact info.

The Preproduction Process

There's a lot that goes into finding the right location. If you don't have a location professional with you, take the director or the AD. They'll know what equipment is needed for the shoot and whether or not the location you're scouting can accommodate it.

You'll also want to make sure you can do as many shoots as possible in a given location. The major locations will be the most important. Imagine that the film you're working on takes place largely in a Victorian-style home. Find the principle location first, as most of your shooting will take place there. Because you will be using that location for a lot of the shooting, you can put more budget toward needed alterations or repairs.

Very-large-budget films can sometimes afford to alter a building, a house, a lot or anything else they need substantially. For low-budget films, look for locations that require as little alteration as possible. If you need a run-down trailer court for some scenes, look for a run-down trailer court to shoot in. Don't get a bunch of old trailers, build a set and dress each one for the perfect look. It will eat up budget. Only splurge on sets that are necessary to tell the story.

Sometimes They Want Too Much

Some location owners will want far too much from the film production in exchange for using their home. They may want a large sum of money for using the location, too much guaranteed in repairs—if needed—and a lot of accommodations that won't make it work.

Remember, there is always somewhere else.

INT and EXT

Just because a script says that scenes take place in the interior and exterior of a building, doesn't mean you have to shoot those scenes in the same building or outside of it. You can get exterior establishing shots and then use a studio for the interior shots. This allows you to set it up however you want without having to alter a location to accommodate shooting and can be far less expensive.

Consider the Little Things

It's easy to scout locations and to miss some glaring problems. Let's use the period film example again. In the average home of the period that is now a modern-day house, you'll have to deal with the following:

- *Removing or hiding any modern trappings: wall art, phone jacks, network jacks, etc.;*
- *Staircases and other obstacles to equipment.*
- *Modern finishes such as high-efficiency windows. There's nothing like accidentally having a triple-pane, clearly modern window in a shot that's supposed to take place in the late 1800s!*
- *Lighting. This may need to be altered considerably. Modern lighting fixtures may have to be removed;*
- *Fireplaces may be bricked up for safety, but may have to be restored to get the authentic look;*
- *Heating grates may need to be changed or removed;*
- *Walls may need to be repainted or at least treated with a dingy look as was characteristic of homes with coal heat.*

There are plenty of little issues like these that you'll have to deal with. If they become numerous, it will result in a detrimental outcome for your budget. Consider this: If you see too many little things that have to be altered, check out another location. If you run into those same issues, you may need a creative solution to a universal problem that you'll have to deal with.

Remember When

Most homeowners will be thrilled to have a film shot at their house. Keep in mind that you are inconveniencing them. Make sure you can give them a firm date as to when you'll need the home so that they can clear out. Some homeowners may want to hang around and watch and, as long as they're not a distraction or an obstacle, this can be acceptable. If you need them to clear out and they're a bit put off by that, you can always explain the fact that films need to have a lot of confidentiality and that you cannot risk anyone learning anything about the film until it's ready to be marketed. If they're crowding your production and insist on hanging out to watch—and provide a distraction—find somewhere else.

A Note on Planning

When you see a film production crew roll into a neighborhood, it becomes apparent how involved these operations are. It involves several trucks, lots of cable and equipment, plenty of people, temporary tents where the crew and cast can eat and so forth.

The closer one location is to another, the better it is. This can cut down on your budget. If you do have to use locations that are far away from one another, be sure that your scheduling accommodates this, which is discussed in the upcoming section.

One way to cut down on your costs is to draw a circle on your map of the city. Find your primary location is and set a radius to work within. Draw a circle that corresponds to a 5 mile radius of the principle location and start scouting within that boundary. You'll be grateful when your crew can hop from one location to another without any delays or a lot of driving around.

Scheduling shoots is important. It's not possible to overstate how important it is. In order to keep within your budget and to ensure that your film gets finished within the amount of time you had agreed upon with writers, funders and others, you have to schedule efficiently.

The next chapter will detail how shoots are scheduled and gives resources to help you keep your film on track.

References

http://gawker.com/5196154/how-movie-stars-get-paid

http://www.imdb.com/news/ni46840810/

http://locationmanagers.org/lmga/

http://www.filmslatemagazine.com/filmmaking/is-your-script-ready

http://www.dga.org/

Chapter 4

Scheduling Shoots

Scheduling shoots is an art in and of itself. A great producer can do it so that there is minimal hassle for the cast and crew and so that the budget's potential is maximized.

There is software available that can help with this. Gorilla is one of the popular options, as is Movie Magic. Either of these can be an invaluable resource, so consider getting software right from the start.

No matter what software you are using, the scheduling process will be difficult. You'll have to make sure that you have all the information you need in place to get it right. This information starts with a script breakdown, which can be put together by you and the director or the AD and the director. Since it's such an important part of the scheduling process, the script breakdown bears further explanation. Coming up with the storyboards is also a part of this process in many productions, so that is detailed in the next section, .

The Script Breakdown
After you've taken out all of the unnecessary elements from the script, it will be reduced to a, hopefully great, story. Within that story are myriad details. Consider this very simple scene: A man is

standing in his kitchen with a voiceover providing his inner dialogue. He is toasting bread for breakfast. To break down this scene, you will assemble the following list of required items:

- *A toaster;*
- *Bread;*
- *Cast members required;*
- *Coffee cups;*
- *Coffee pot;*
- *Crew members required;*
- *Flatware and silverware;*
- *Lighting;*
- *The man's clothing, item by item;*
- *Wardrobe required.*

As the producer, your role is to make sure that everything is in place for the scene to happen. This means that you have to be detailed. The last thing you want is to consistently have scenes run over budget because the crew has to look for items that weren't listed on the shooting script.

You'll also want to include information from the director about how the scene should play out, the mood, and so forth. This will feed into the shooting script but, first, it feeds into the budget.

The script breakdown is an invaluable budgeting tool. The breakdown lets you know which props you need, which crewmembers will need to be paid that day, whether or not the shoot will be long enough that there needs to be catering, and so forth. Each scene should have a budget associated with it.

Once the scene is properly broken down, you assign to it a number. This number will remain consistent thought the production process. If the above scene were Scene 3, , and an additional scene needed to be placed before it, it would be Scene 2B. This prevents having to renumber scenes that, even on a small production, can cause a lot of confusion and headaches.

TIP: Scripts will be revised and reissued constantly throughout a production. Be sure you have and that you stick to a numbering system that everyone will understand. The following system works very well.

When you add a scene after an established scene, designate it with an appended letter, not a new number, as explained above. If another scene is added between a new scene and one from the original script, append another letter, but leave the number the same. For example:

- *Original scene order: Scene 1, 2, 3;*
- *Adding a scene after 2 and before 3: 1, 2, 2A, 3;*
- *Adding a scene after 2 and 2A: 1, 2, 2A, 2Aa, 3.*

There are various ways that you can make this work, but be sure it's consistent.

Once you have a breakdown for every scene, you can start deciding on how you're going to budget your money for all the various scenes that you're going to have to shoot. This process can be vital to keeping within a budget and, sometimes, it means making some painful cuts.

Understanding Budgeting and Scenes

Because we're not talking about a huge production, you will be have to be frugal with your budget. This sometimes means that certain scenes will have to be cut out altogether as you do your breakdown. You may find that some scenes will end up costing so much to shoot that you'll go over budget simply by giving them the most basic treatment.

For example, imagine that your script has scenes in it that take place at night. Night shots are more expensive due to the lighting required, the generators for that lighting, having the crew work late hours and so forth. You would have two budget-saving options here.

If the fact that the scene takes place at night makes no difference to the story—remember, films are stories and that's the most important thing to keep in mind when going through this process—you may be able to convert it to a day scene. In one change from "EXT – NIGHT" to "EXT – DAY," you've saved the costs of the lighting, late-night crew hours and the expenses that arise from the sheer difficulty of shooting at night.

If the scene must take place at night, you can opt for a day-for-night shot. If you have a good director and good camera operators, this can be very effective and it can be easier on the audience, as you can bring out the elements of the shot that need to be seen and hide some imperfections by darkening those parts of the frame that do not need to be seen.

With the advent of digital effects, low-budget film producers have a tremendous resource that they can call upon to enhance these effects and sell them to the audience. A good CGI artist can change the lighting in a scene enough to make light shadows into impenetrable blacks and can highlight elements such as the light coming out of a window to make it stand out from the ambient light, even if the original shot was taken during the day.

There will be changes to the breakdown when you make these types of alterations. , if you're going to do day-for-night, you'll need to increase the light levels of some elements, such as lights coming through the windows on a house. This means a small change. The 60W incandescent that was originally going to be shining through the window from a practical light might be changed to a halogen to make it stand out against the daylight.

Many other techniques can be used to pull off this particular effect. Other effects may be used and this can cut down on the budget considerably, allowing for a very convincing film at a much lower price than may have been possible if every shot were simply put together in the most obvious way, i.e. shooting night shots at night.

Reducing the Shoot Schedule Though Consolidation

Let's continue with the above example. You have a series of night shots and have decided to use day-for-night to cut down on the costs of filming. You can take this one step further and bring down the budget.

To do so, you would schedule these shots to be contiguous. If they have to be shot over the course of several days, you can still save on your budget by making sure you schedule them to be shot on consecutive days. This allows the crew to have things more or less in place at the beginning of the shooting day, saving a lot of time on setting up the same gear over and over again. It also allows for consistency between the various shots, given that as little as possible will have changed between the individual scenes being filmed.

You'll find that, as you break down the script, a lot of scenes that don't follow one another in the story most certainly should in the schedule. I f you're watching a spy thriller, you can be sure that all the scenes shot in the villain's lair were shot back-to-back, even if the shots don't appear close to one another in the film.

You can also consolidate scenes that are written to take place in different locations to take place in the same location, if it suits the story. For example, if you have a movie where there are scenes of teenagers in school and of them walking home through their neighborhood, you may be able to replace the neighborhood scenes with scenes of them walking through the hallways at school. This could cut down on transportation costs, crew costs, the time involved in shooting, the time involved in permitting, clearing and preparing the neighborhood location. It eliminates the need to even scout a neighborhood to shoot in at all.

As you're breaking down your script, look for areas where you could combine scenes into the same location. This oftentimes doesn't at all detract from the quality of the film. Sometimes, it makes the film better, putting focus on the characters and the story.

Consolidating scenes can also be done based on which members of the cast are on-set on a particular day. The idea is to cut out as many days of shooting as possible, which brings down the budget. Anything you can do to accomplish this is usually worth it. There are some cases where it won't be possible, but more where it is entirely workable.

As you break down the script, start looking for scenes, props, sets and other resources that are common across many scenes. Use this as a way to group shoots together when you get to scheduling.

Once you have a good spec script and a breakdown of the project, start looking for a director, if you don't have one attached already. The next chapter will help you to understand how that's best done.

Making a Shooting Script

This will require input from the director, as anything the director wants indicated on the shooting script should be there. It makes their job easier. This script is not intended for any type of pitch. A completed shooting script is a very technical document—and a living document—so it's not at all suitable as a way to pitch your story. This is the script that contains as much information about the shoot as possible, what's required for the shoot, what camera angles are required and so forth.

Shooting scripts aren't pretty. They are more or less standardized, though some directors, producers, and other high-up individuals within the filmmaking process may have customizations that they want. The following information will detail what's on a shooting scripts and formatting conventions.

Scene Numbers

As discussed earlier, scene numbers need to be assigned and they need to follow a convention. You'll have done this during the breakdown process.

Headings

Headings on shooting scripts are standardized. Your director and the rest of the crew will expect three pieces of information to be on this part of the script, so be sure that all three are there. They are:

- *Interior or Exterior, most commonly abbreviated INT and EXT;*
- *Where the shot is taking place;*
- *What time of day the shot is taking place at;*
- *This format is not only standardized, it is simplified. This means that it is either:*
  - *INT or EXT;*
  - *DAY or NIGHT.*

The location line depends upon your script. HANGAR BAY should always refer to the location known as HANGAR BAY in every other instance where it is mentioned.

As an example:

INT - HANGAR BAY – DAY

Each scene in the film should have its own heading, even if the scenes follow one another in the narrative and are shot in the same location at the same time of day. Again, this is to eliminate the chances that confusion will lead to wasted time and money.

There are some other headings that are used in shooting scripts. The important thing is to make sure that they don't gets so varied between one and the next that it causes confusion. To indicate that the action is moving between two established times and locations, , you can use "INTERCUT." If you want to follow a character from their bedroom to the front door and back to the bedroom, you can use "BACK TO" when they head back to the bedroom to indicate that it's a different scene in the same location.

Oftentimes, specify a date and time in a scene, particularly if it's important to the narrative. Information relevant to the time, place and narrative of a story do belong up on the header, positioned wherever you think appropriate, but definitely part of the header. For example: "JULY 4, 1776 EXT – HENRY'S FRONT PORCH – DAY"

The Narrative
When screenwriters put too much technical direction into spec scripts, it tends to be mixed in with the narrative of the scene. The narrative describes what is going on, visually and aurally, in the scene.

This will generally already be a part of the spec script and you'll likely have to clean it up a bit to remove information that's already there. There are two main criteria for whether or not something belongs in the narrative parts of the shooting script. These criteria are:

- *The audience can see it;*
- *The audience can hear it.*

Post-Production

There are no other ways in which audiences interact with films, at least on the physical level. This is all the information that the director needs.

The descriptions of how the actors in the film feel are generally given in terms of how they look. Someone can be "looking into the mirror, eyes wide with fear," but "she's feeling fear" wouldn't normally be in the narrative.

All of this is put together to create the directions for shooting a given scene. Character names, important props, and important directions are oftentimes written in ALL CAPS to denote that they are vital to the scene. Below is an example of an actual shooting script, from the film *Memento*, as reproduced by Daily Script

1   INT. DERELICT HOUSE - DAY   1

A POLAROID PHOTOGRAPH, clasped between finger and thumb: a crude, crime scene flash picture of a MAN'S BODY lying on a decaying wooden floor, a BLOODY MESS where his head should be.

The image in the photo starts to FADE as we SUPER TITLES. The hand holding the photo suddenly FANS it in a rapid FLAPPING motion, then holds it still. The image fades more, and again the picture is FANNED.

As TITLES END the image fades to nothing. The hand holding the photo FLAPS it again, then places it at the front of a POLAROID CAMERA.

The camera SUCKS the blank picture up, then the FLASH BURSTS.

Note the formatting. The first piece of information on the page is the scene number, as this is the most vital piece of information and the one the director will want first. The Heading gives INT/EXT, LOCATION and TIME information.

The block of text that follows is the narrative. It's describing what the audience sees and hears, including the transition involving the film titles.

Important directions, prop names and other information is set in ALL CAPS so that the director and rest of the crew know that this is vital.

Format
Most of the formatting already know, but here are some basic conventions for formatting shooting scripts.

- *Headings, vital direction, props and character names are ALL CAPS;*
- *Narrative is otherwise written according to standard English convention;*
- *Scene numbers are standardized throughout the shooting scripts;*
- *When a script is revised, a new page is issued with an asterisk in the right margin of the page next to all changed lines;*
- *Revised pages are also printed on different colored paper so that everyone can be sure they're looking at the same material;*
- *If a script needs so much revision that rewriting it entirely makes sense, the scenes will usually be renumbered;*
- *If a scene is omitted, it is left in the script with the designation OMITTED appearing on the headline;*
- *The date of the revision is included on the top of the page, along with the color code for the revision. : REVISED 10/10/12 BLUE.*

Colors
Shooting scripts are constantly revised during any production process. Whenever a page is revised, it is distributed on colored

paper. Each new revision of a page should be done on a new color of paper. If the same color is used twice due to many revisions, it is called the "double" of the color. The second time green is used, , the revised pages would be referred to as double green.

There's no need to worry about a convention here. If you want to move from white to yellow to blue, that's entirely acceptable. The only thing that matters is that this convention is used to ensure that people aren't confused as to which version of a scene they should be looking at.

Storyboard

Creating storyboards allows you to get an idea of what each shot will look like once it is completed. The artwork on these does not have to be ornate. There are professionals who can produce storyboards that are as high-quality as comic books but, sometimes, all that's needed are basic outlines of the items in the scene, the characters in the scene and how the shot needs to be framed.

Storyboards are useful tools for keeping budgets down. Rather than shooting scenes that don't end up working out as desired, the storyboarding process allows each idea for a scene to be analyzed, changed, and decided upon before the shooting process starts.

Here's how the process works.

Match Your Format
Make certain that the storyboard format matches the format for your film. If you're shooting in HD, then the storyboards should be proportioned accordingly. If you're shooting on 35mm, use the same proportions as the film.

There are readymade storyboarding notebooks that you can purchase. If you have ideas for a shot, this is a great way to communicate them. The storyboards that you'll use for the actual shoot need to be more sophisticated.

Storyboards traditionally have a border that denotes the edges of the screen. Underneath this will be enough room to write a description of the action in the scene. The scene number needs to be located somewhere at the top of the storyboard, so that the right storyboard is associated with the right scene in the shooting script.

The storyboards are developed from the shooting script and are good ways to test shots. They can also be excellent tools for accurately predicting potential overruns in the budget.

Imagine that a scene involves a character with a magical, glowing wizard staff. Every time that staff appears on camera, it means that a special effect has to be used to make the glowing effect. Using storyboards, it's possible to figure out good shots that deliberately leave it off camera, bringing down the effects budget.

Assembling the Schedule

Here's where things come together. You now have your shooting script and a storyboard, which together should prepare you to shoot every scene in the film. Each of those scenes will have a specific location, and that gives you the first piece of information you need. Avoid multiple trips to the same location during the production. Ideally, you'll be able to film every scene at a given location consecutively.

The aforementioned software, Gorilla, Movie Magic and any others, are preferable to the old technique of using a production board. The volume of information that the producer must create, store, update and distribute requires a computer. Get some software and you'll be very glad you made the move when your production starts to get very expensive and involved.

If you're using software, it will give you several appearance options. You can also use templates in programs such as Microsoft Word. The shooting schedule should contain:

- *The date and time;*

- *The location at which the shoot will take place;*
- *The scenes that are to be shot;*
- *The people who are required to be at the shoot;*
- *The equipment required to complete the shoot.*

Some shooting schedules get very complex. You may want to include specific information on the schedule such as when the location will be safety-checked, which pages of the script are being used, and so forth. Information on breakdown sheets and how you can use them are included at the end of this section.

Loose Ends

You won't get everything shot on the schedule you set, the quality level you expect, and within the timeframe you mandated. This simply will not happen. Accept that there will be finish up work and you can start thinking rationally rather than being frustrated by an inevitability as the production unfolds.

Deal with this by scheduling pickup shoots. These shoots can be scheduled at any time. They can be added to weeks when production is still ongoing but, quite frequently, they end up being shot after filming has officially ended.

You may also find out that something in the story doesn't work and need to add scenes after the movie is finished. This is workable.

For production, it's important that everyone does their best to hold up their obligation to stay on schedule and to make sure the production goes as smoothly as possible. It's also important to remember that mistakes do happen. These should be considered in your budget and anticipated at least a couple of days of pickup shooting on top of your regular shooting schedule. If the film happens to have a very long shooting schedule, there may be even more pickup shoots that need to be scheduled.

Be ready for unexpected problems and anticipate that there will be some material that needs to be shot for the film after the post-production process has started.

Your Breakdown Sheet

The producers and the higher-ups in the production will want more detail at their fingertips about every scene that's being shot. There are various ways that you can do this, but the best way is to print out a sheet for each scene and include it with the information that is handed out to the appropriate person. The sheet should be a conglomerate sheet that includes all the information that specific departments would have, but that would only be all gathered together on one sheet for the people with the most responsibility for the production. They should include, at least:

- *Wardrobe: What items are needed that day.*
- *Stunts: What stunts are being performed and by whom;*
- *Props: Which props are used in each scene;*
- *Actors: Which actors are in each scene;*
- *Extras: How many there are;*
- *Special effects: Give a summary of the effect to be employed;*
- *Vehicles;*
- *Animals;*
- *Special personnel;*
- *Additional information: Are streets blocked off for the production; is cold weather gear or rain gear required for the crew; etc.*

This allows the people who need to make sure that everything is in place to do so quickly and easily.

If you're using a software product, this is much easier. They have templates that allow you to print out these sheets very easily and that are set up so that you don't have to figure it all out manually.

After you have the shoot scheduled, you will have a very good handle on how much of your budget will go toward the actual shooting of the film. You can accurately determine the budget for each day and add a bit more for pickup shoots. This is the end of the production process. From here on out, you will be working on the locations that you scouted, using the props and costumes you bought, and putting the actors on film.

References
http://www.videomaker.com/article/10368-shooting-day-for-night

Chapter 5

The Production Process Begins

The production process is one of the most stressful, and one of the most exciting, parts of the entire process of filmmaking. When people show filmmaking in movies and in television, this is the part of it that they usually show. They don't show the agonizing work of finding people for a film, setting a budget, scheduling shoots and so forth. What they show is the *"lights, camera, action"* phase of film production. They do that because it can be incredible, if it comes off right and if it's well coordinated.

Here's how it comes together. When it's done right, it is why films are among the most popular forms of entertainment in history.

Know Your Limitations

This phase of the project is where your crew and cast decisions are going to pay off or cost you. If you did well selecting a crew, you will be sending a well-oiled machine out on every day they're scheduled to shoot. The shoots will be done on time and within budget. The scenes that need to be shot will be shot and the performances will all be excellent.

Then again, films are made in the real world, and that's hardly ever how things turn out.

The production process, not surprisingly, is the part of the process where the producer is needed most of all. The producer will keep an eye on everything, make sure that all the work is getting done and make sure that everyone is doing their jobs to the highest standards.

To do this, a producer has to accept their limitations. You can't be everywhere and you can't possibly keep track of everything that's going on at the shooting locations. Here are some tips for dealing with the difficulties that will arise from the fact that you are simply a human being.

Delegating

As far as making sure the shoots happen as they're supposed to, your director is your right-hand man or woman. This is the person that can take the script and turn it into something marvelous on film—or video—with a combination of technical knowledge and aesthetic sensibility.

Rely on your director to make sure that anything you need done on the shoots gets done. If you decide that he or she is going over budget, be able to count on their input to tell you how to avoid that without significantly compromising the film. If a cast member doesn't measure up to your expectations, the director should be able to get the performance out of them that you need.

Your director will have their AD to rely upon, so remember that working with your director, in some ways, is like working with a team. Be sure you coordinate with them understanding that they may delegate tasks, as it makes it possible for them to do more for you and for the production.

Department Heads
Your lead makeup, wardrobe, set dressers and other personnel have to be able to hold up their ends. They shouldn't be contacting you with every minor problem or to tell you that they never have enough money.

They should also be able to delegate within their own departments. For example, if the director decides that the hero wardrobe isn't quite right for a certain scene, the head of your costuming department should be able to, with the help of their own people, make whatever changes are needed without it turning into a fiasco. Having staff who can sew, they should be able to alter or change anything as long as the request is within reason and they have access to necessary materials.

Crew
Your grips, gaffers, swing gang and so forth all have to be reliable people. On low-budget films, it's sometimes very budget-friendly to go around to local film schools and to hire people on as interns or for their first jobs. If you go this route, make sure that the people you hire on are capable of doing their jobs without constant supervision or correction. You'll save time on shoots and get better results. A $400,000 to $5,000,000 film may not be a huge production, but it's a serious budget at either end of that spectrum and some novices are not quite ready to work under the demands and pressure that the budget will make inevitable.

Cast
Some actors are so good at their craft that they deserve a bit of extra attention here and there. Some actors need certain conditions to be met so that they can get into character and turn out a great performance.

There are other actors who like to think they are the former, but are prima donnas. These types can turn into real headaches.

If the cast cannot provide the performances you need, you may have to reshoot parts of the film. If there is a problem, this is why it's important to catch it right away. Actors are artists, yes, but they're also professionals and, if they cannot perform their jobs, they need to be replaced.

Actors that are very demanding, rude to crew and other workers, and who otherwise make productions unpleasant can disrupt a production to the point where nothing goes right. It's important to keep egos in check on a film set and as a producer, you and your director may have to occasionally do this to an actor that's a bit too impressed with their own potential.

Some actors are so well-known and so likely to bring in receipts that it makes it worth anything to work with them. If you have access to such an actor, their salability may make it worth a few temper tantrums here and there.

Hiring a Line Producer

You can hire a line producer from the film's top crew or you can hire one as a separate crew member. Either way, they can be enormously helpful. Sometimes they mean the difference between a film that stays within budget and one that goes over.

What Do They Do?

Line producers act in the place of a producer during the shoot. They also assist during the preproduction process and during post-production, in many cases. These are your go-to source for everything. It's not an easy job but, for some people, it's something that they do very well. That makes them tremendously valuable to film productions.

As far as the day-to-day operations of the shoot go, the line producer handles pretty much everything that the producer would handle. They take care of budget issues, they have influence on the actual outcome of the film, and they make sure that everyone and everything needed shows up at the shoots.

A good line producer can take a lot of stress off the producer of a film. They need to be someone the producer can trust and someone with a lot of experience in the filmmaking business. If you're looking to your own crew, the AD is a good choice for this job. If you're looking outside of your crew, look for an experienced line producer or someone who has a lot of set experience and understands the specifics of what needs to get done. Producers are another potential source, as they may want to expand their experience by working under another producer.

Hiring Unit Production Managers

Unit production managers can be incredible assets. They work under the line producer, the producer and the director. They are also known as production supervisors or as production managers, though unit production manager is the official term for this job.

The unit production manager handles budget concerns that have to do with the items such as equipment, locations, and so forth. They will also deal with the crew on the film that functions below the department heads.

The unit production manager is a manager in every sense of the word. They don't make changes to shots, they don't have any say in the film, but they do have a lot to do with the success or failure of the film in many regards. They make sure that budgets are accommodated and that the work necessary gets done at the levels below the director and line producer's direct concerns.

The unit production manager will help with finding locations. He or shee will make sure that reports are filed as needed, make sure that permits are taken care of and so forth. The PM also makes sure that the cast and crew have a way to get to the filming location, coordinates with local authorities if special accommodations are required—street closures, etc.—and makes sure that every item required for the shoots is considered in the budget.

These are very valuable crewmembers. They fill an important role in the way a producer delegates authority, allowing a production to run more smoothly. These professionals are represented by the DGA, so there are salary requirements and other union mandated concessions, if the film is a union one. They may add to the budget in terms of their salaries, but their skills can make up for that cost by keeping a film within budget.

If you're looking for someone to handle this work, look for a unit production manager with impeccable organizational skills and an ability to motivate team members to carry out the directives of higher-ups. The director or line producer may have suggestions for people whom they've worked with in the past who do this job very well.

Working with Budgets

If you've done a good job budgeting your film you can expect to get great results within the budget that you've set. If not, you're going to see the results of poor budgeting in the outcome of your film.

During the filming process, there will likely be occasions when you run over budget and some happy occasions where you run under. Ideally, this would all balance out and you would be well within your lines. What if you're not?

First, Track It

The worst thing you can do is take yourself out of the financial loop. Your unit production manager and line producers should be giving you daily figures on any overruns in the budget. You can do this on the Movie Magic software or your can do this manually. If you want to keep things as simple as possible, use a spreadsheet program and have the managers and line producer update the figures whenever required. It's very easy to get this set up so that everyone can work off of the same sheet, no matter where they are.

Second, Ask the Director

The director has control of the creative aspects of the film. That means that they have control over a lot of the money and how it's spent, . If you have a good director, you can usually work out these problems.

If the director insists that a shot needs to be done in a way that will make it more expensive than projected, you might be able to accommodate this by asking them where they could cut back.

If one scene is causing the problem, this is easy enough to deal with. Another scene might be cut out or altered to fix the problem with the money. If the budget problems are related to the director consistently making artistic decisions that do not support the budget, then there's a problem. You'll have to make the director understand that resources are limited and that every scene cannot serve artistic choices that aren't financially realistic.

Third, Look at Other Costs

Some cost overruns occur simply because things turned out to be more expensive than the original estimate. Look at costs for food, space, construction, and so forth. You may be able to take care of it by shifting some services around or cutting back on some.

Cutting Scenes Back

Cutting back on a scene or even eliminating it is a huge decision. It's one that the producer will likely make along with the director, AD, and other people at the top of the production. Here are some things to consider about doing this:

- *Does it affect the continuity of the film? Check with the script supervisor;*
- *Does it contribute significantly to the film? Check to be sure, as most scripts have a few scenes that could go;*
- *A scene with many extras and set pieces that isn't necessary is a natural choice for removal to save on budget.*

If the budget overrun is related to the location, consider relocating the shoot to somewhere more affordable. If the film is renting the interior of a theater for a shoot, the purpose of the scene may be served just as well if it was shot in a different location, such as a studio lot.

Notice that today many DVDs come with deleted scenes that never made it into the finished film. If you're good, you can cut out scenes that would be on the cutting room floor, anyway, and save all the time and money involved with shooting them. If you're having a hard time deciding what to let go, review the script. Look for scenes where the audience will to get bored and where the plot isn't advanced. For example:

- *Scenes with a lot of exposition that is redundant or boring;*
- *Scenes that introduce minor plot points that don't affect the outcome of the story;*
- *Subplots that go nowhere; you can cut out a lot of scenes by getting rid of these;*
- *Scenes that have a lot of special effects requirements but aren't necessary. For example, in a horror film, you might be able to cut down on the special effects gore without making the film any less scary;*
- *Scenes that might change the rating of the film to one that you don't want. If you're shooting for PG-13, look for the harsh scenes that push the limits. If you're shooting for R, look for the things that would make the MPAA give it an NC-17.*

Remember that one of the most important processes that a film goes through and that can make a mediocre film great is editing. It's sometimes in cutting away the fat that the real meat of the story is revealed.

Also keep in mind that it's sometimes more effective not to show a low-budget rendition of a scene and to reference it in the narrative and make its significance apparent through the performances. For example, if a character in a film has PTSD from being in a major battle during a war, you could easily cut out an expensive battle scene without losing that aspect. What the audience envisions may be more horrible than what you can represent on-screen and might be more effective.

Instead of thinking of cuts as impediments to your vision, think of them as surgeries that get rid of things you don't want, ensuring the health of the film on the whole.

Going Over Budget

Going over budget on a production is par for the course in Hollywood. On very large productions, it's likely that the producer can always get more funding to finish the project, since so much will to have been invested in it already.

For smaller films, going over budget can be a major issue. Remember that going over budget during the shooting phase means that you have less money for post-production, marketing and everything else. You need that money but, sometimes, you're not going to have enough to cover the costs of the film that you're working on.

Keep in mind that spending more money doesn't necessarily mean that you'll get a better, or more profitable, film. Hollywood is famous for its many instances of excessive over-budget spending. Hollywood is equally notable for having produced many expensive bombs.

If you're going to go over budget, be prepared to go through some real pain.

Many film studios will demand that you get a lower fee for your services if you're the producer and you go over budget. You may, in essence, pay for it out of your own pocket, which gives you a good incentive to keep within budget.

If you're working with a studio or financiers who regularly fund films, will not be allowed to go over your budget and that's the whole of the situation. You'll have to cut somewhere.

Remember that going over budget can ruin an entire production. This is why hiring line producers and unit production managers is essential. Keep an eye on the money at the most granular levels and things stay within cost.

If you believe in the project and the director does, too, you might be able to finish an over-budget production by reducing your fees. Remember that if you're going over budget consistently during the production process, your budget for everything else is reduced. Things are only going to get worse as the project unfolds.

Surprises vs. Incompetence
Shooting a film is always going to be a process rife with surprises. There will be days when the shooting schedule has been done perfectly, everyone shows up, and the crew is perfectly professional, but the weather refuses to cooperate, blowing budget. There will be times when an actor will get ill or have another issue that makes it impossible for them to perform. Surprises happen all the time.

Budget overruns are usually surprises, but when you start being less surprised that they happened and more familiar with the sensation of having to deal with them, you might recognize incompetence on the part of the cast or crew that you have to deal with.

Find Where It's Coming From
Is the director reshooting every scene because it never seems to turn out? Is the on-set sound consistently too bad to be used? Is the wardrobe always late or the makeup bad?

These are signs that someone is incompetent at their job. Their incompetence may be due to lack of experience or care, or it may be due to the fact that they're not getting the support they need to do their jobs correctly. Whatever the cause may be, you have to root it out.

Some producers will go ballistic. The filmmaking industry is one that's rather famous—or infamous—for being the chosen industry of some very hot-headed individuals. Other producers will be more methodical and less temperamental when ironing out problems with the cast or crew, or letting people go.

Whatever works best for you is always the right route here. Remember: If you're over budget, you'll be the proud producer of a project that never made it to completion because you couldn't handle a budget. It's not good for your reputation.

Big Concerns for Producers

Being realistic, there will be too many crew members and cast for you to keep track of completely. Most of the big concerns you'll have will be ones that you'll address along with the help of the people who share the top positions on the films.

If there's a problem with the boom operator, you can talk to the head of the sound department and they'll make sure it gets taken care of. If you have trouble with a department head, you can talk to the line producer and they'll sort it out. If you have a problem with the director, it's all on you.

If you have a problem with the director's work, remember that the director is the one who controls the creative aspects of the film. If they're good, they want to make sure you're producing the film you set out to produce and won't try to take over the entire production.

If the film isn't turning out the way you envisioned, take a look at these areas first:

Direction

If the direction is bad, everything else may be bad. Other than the producer blowing the budget, the director is the person with the highest likelihood of ruining a film.

There are some characteristic signs of bad direction. It's not as obvious as the signs of having a bad cinematographer..

What Happened?

A director, in some senses, directs the audience as well as the film through the story that the film is trying to tell. They take all the shots, all the sound and all the special effects and put them together into a coherent story that the audience can follow.

If you're watching the film and you can't tell what's happening or why it's important, it's a sign that the director may not be doing a good job. Given that you'll know the script inside and out, the story should be familiar to you. If the film makes it less clear, you may have a problem.

Where Is This?

Good directors always make sure the audience understands where they are. In *Raiders of the Lost Ark*, the protagonist goes from an ancient temple to a runway to a fight that takes place across several vehicles and the audience never loses track of him. In lesser films, the audience may not be able to tell that the characters are moving from place to place, or the director may never even establish that different interiors are in different locations in the story. Spielberg manages to establish this.

Bad Blocking

Blocking refers to how the actors stand and move around the shot. Actors have to be given a chance to rehearse so that their movement is natural and convincing on the screen.

When a director isn't blocking scenes properly, the effects can be very noticeable. People will move unnaturally or constantly be standing in the same place. Oftentimes, this results in very awkward performances.

Bad Scenes Left In

If you want to see the worst possible results of someone not reshooting bad scenes, you can refer to Ed Wood films, such as *Plan 9 from Outer Space*. Bad scenes that should be reshot include:

- *Scenes where flaws in the set are visible;*
- *Scenes where the action is not moving quickly enough;*
- *Scenes in which there are obvious continuity errors, such as candles getting longer as they burn;*
- *Scenes where there are anachronisms, such as a part of a car or a modern door lock being visible in a period film.*

Sadly, a few of these types of scenes left in a finished film can make it into a laughing stock. Imagine if an extra wearing jeans and a T-shirt was visible in *Titanic* or if you saw someone's finger manipulating the space ships in the climactic battle of *Star Wars*. Everything that was great about those films would be ruined in a second or less.

If there are errors in the film that make it look unprofessional, point them out and don't go with the "no one will notice" excuse. They will.

Insist on a reshoot if the scene is vital to the film. If the scene can be dispensed with altogether, it's better to get rid of it than leave it in.

Low-budget films have some margin of forgiveness among audiences in this regard. , *Halloween* contains numerous scenes that have problems that take away from the film, but it's still a very popular and beloved film. Unless your film is that noteworthy though, audiences are likely to be rather unforgiving if it looks unprofessional or even silly.

Bad Performances
Sometimes, a producer will sign actors only to find out that they're not quite as good as the producer originally thought. This is unavoidable. However, it is unusual to have an entire cast that is giving bad performances, even if they're not terribly experienced film actors.

This may come down to the direction. If the director consistently fails to inspire actors give better performances, you'll end up with a subpar film.

Be sure the director is communicating what the cast needs to know to give great performances. If they don't seem to be very into their characters, it might be because the director isn't providing what the actors need to breathe life into those characters.

Inconsistency
If you take a look at great films, they tend to have a cohesive look and feel to them throughout. This ensures that there aren't jarring moments for the audience and it ensures that the audience can settle into the feel of the film.

If the look and feel of the film is changing throughout in a nonsensical way, bring it up. A director may start getting very dark or become very lighthearted in their direction style, even though the film wasn't intended to go that way. Ultimately such creative choices will affect the film's style.

The Shots Don't Fit the Characters
This problem is easy to illustrate. If Peter Jackson had continually shot Frodo from *Lord of the Rings* from a low angle, he would look tall. The point of his character was his unassuming physicality.

Make sure the director is shooting the characters correctly. It shouldn't be obvious that the villain after the damsel in distress is inches shorter than her. A powerful, warrior character should not be shot in a way that makes him look lumpy and small. A debutante shouldn't look like she works her biceps 8 hours per day. Poor choices in directing the shots can cause these, and other, problems.

The director, to a great extent, tells the story through the way that they set up the shots. If the shots don't portray the characters faithfully to how they're written, the audience won't feel what they should.

Someone Is Getting Special Attention
Does the director have a friend in the cast who is getting too much attention? Look for scenes where the camera lingers on someone who isn't doing anything. Look for scenes when someone delivers a line in a way that makes it look like they've seen acting, but never practiced it.

From time to time, someone on your crew—including the director—might decide to do someone a favor by giving them a break. Where directors are concerned, they sometimes get fixated on a performer and keep including them in their films, even though the performer is detracting from their work.

Too…Something
Some directors have a characteristic style. J.J. Abrams, the director of the latest *Star Trek* movies, likes light and a lot of light flares in his shots. This works well for him. Every good director will have things that are common throughout their films.

Sometimes they go a bit too far with this and it can take away from the film. If you start noticing a lot of signature shots, that don't serve the style or mood of the film, point them out. The film isn't about the director, but some directors like to star in films from behind the camera.

Ego

Directors understand that creativity, drive, vision, and commitment make great films. Producers understand that all of those things can be represented as funds the producer needs to raise to pay for them.

If the director is getting too carried away with the importance of their vision—or the importance of themselves—the producer has to keep them in check. Don't be afraid to remind your director that they work for you and for the film. They can't get their way all the time, and they can't be abusive when they don't. If every decision you make turns into an argument with the director—or if the director is openly disparaging you— let them go.

Cameras

It doesn't take a genius to figure out that having trouble with your cameras or camera operators will be detrimental to a film. If the director isn't the cause of bad results, it might be that they're not working with a good DP. The people you'll be concerned with if the cinematography is a problem are:

- *The DP;*
- *The camera operator;*
- *The assistants.*

Do you have the right people working the camera? You can have the best DP in the world, but if they're working with an incompetent operator and crew, there's no way they can give you what you're after and, in all likelihood, they're irritated, too.

Lighting

Lighting on a film set is not an easy job. This is handled by the DP, the gaffers and the grips.

If the lighting is bad, it might be that the gaffers and the grips aren't doing their jobs right. You may have actors that aren't lit properly and that can ruin a scene. If this is happening over and over, there may be a problem that could be fixed by swapping out some of the crew responsible for the lighting.

Sound

Be sure you check the location sound and verify that it was recorded properly. There will be a lot of sound added in the post-production phase, but you'll want sound from the shoot to work with .

You'll also want to watch for one very serious issue that makes it into a lot of films—visible mics. Boom mic operators have to be sure that their equipment is close enough to capture the audio they need, but they also need to be aware if they're dipping into the frame. It's easier to fix this than it was in the past because of digital post-production options, but it's still horribly unprofessional.

The sound department should be aware of all the audio that they have to capture for a scene. Be sure it's getting done to avoid post-production hassles.

Your director, line producer and unit managers should make sure that the shoot is going as planned.

As one last thing, avoid being an absentee producer. Make sure you show up on the set regularly. It's the only way you can know for sure where and how your money is being spent.

Chapter 6

Post-Production

Post-production has changed a lot in the modern world. It used to be largely about processing film and making prints but, with digital technology, that part of the process isn't even a part of productions. Even so, there are some things that you'll still have to do that have not changed that much over time.

To a great extent, post-production is where the film comes together. When you begin the process, you'll have all the shots that make up the script. You'll have to edit them together, finish recording dialogue, and so forth. How you do that will have a huge influence on the finished product.

Getting the Film Finished

If you stuck to your budget during the shooting process, there should be enough funds to finish the film. The process will differ somewhat depending upon whether you shot digitally or on film, or a combination.

Film
Whether or not you shot on film, the final product will be on video. You'll start with processing and printing up the film and then will have it transferred to video. This is technical work and there isn't any creativity involved in it. Arrange to have this done during the preproduction process. Get bids from a companies that provide this service and choose the company that provides the best quality work for the amount allocated in your budget.

Audio Sync
The audio that was recorded during filming will be synchronized with the video so that the basics are all there. This will be augmented during the post-production process.

Dailies
These show the scenes that were filmed on any given day and they're usually distributed on DVD. These are usually available at the end of the shooting day. This will be the time when the producer, director, and other key production staff look at the rough footage and decide if they want them included in the final edit.

Once everything has been assembled and synced, a rough cut of the movie will be created by the editor. Be aware that this is far from the finished product. The main purpose of this cut is to make sure that all the scenes that were called for were shot.

This is the time when you find out that you must arrange some pickup shots, as it's the first time that everything will be assembled in the correct story order.

Most of this work will be highly technical and, as the producer, you're likely not to be that involved until they present you with the entirety of the filmed scenes. This is where the real creative process begins as you'll get to put these scenes together along with the editor and director to create the film that you want out of the footage that you have.

What Look Do You Want?

There are numerous effects that can be added to film during the post-production phase to give it a particular look. The days when you had to shoot the scene with a filter to get more blue in the image are long gone. You add it during editing now and, if you don't like it, you remove it.

There is a much easier way to change the look of a film; changing the frame rate.

Frame Rate

If you're watching a film, there are 24 images flickering across the screen every second. If you're watching video, 29.97 frames of video are flickering across the screen every second.

Despite this seeming like a small difference, it has a major impact on the look of a movie. Film tends to portray motion in a way that audiences are familiar with. On video, even though the motion capture is aided by the higher frame rate, the effect may look cheap compared to film. There's something more realistic about how movement is captured on film that gives it a different feel that makes the movie less involving for some people.

Going with the notion that more is better, Hollywood is starting to use 48 frames per second. This was used on the recent film *The Hobbit* and it didn't go over well. Some audiences felt that it made the film less involving, as it was obvious that the actors were on a set with computer-generated special effects.

Consider this: You can reduce the frame rate of video to get a film look, but it's not that common to go the other way. People sometimes describe the effect of higher frame rates as making a film look like a soap opera.

There is software that can convert standard definition images into an HD-like format. If that's the look you're going for, it can be done.

Modern Editing

Editing is done these days with software. Unless one is trying to make things more difficult and expensive, there is no reason to do it any other way. It allows for a more cost-effective solution and also helps the creative process.

Editing software makes it easy to insert, delete, and reorder scenes however one wishes. The software allows you to do this without trimming a single negative and it allows it to be done instantly. It is a non-destructive solution as you don't have a negative to destroy.

There are several processes that go along with the editing process, so there's more to this than rearranging the shots into the right order. You will:

- *Do the audio post-production, including recording new audio;*
- *Score the film;*
- *Add special effects.*

These are all involved and expensive processes. The decisions you make regarding each one will affect your budget and ultimately, other creative choices.

Starting the Editing

As you assemble the scenes into an entire film, use the process as an opportunity to increase the quality of your end product. This is the part where you trim away the fat from the steak, so to speak. Here are some of the things you can do as a producer to make sure you're getting the results that you want.

Use Your Angles

A good director will have gotten plenty of angles and extra shots that you can use. This is the time to use them.

Look for how each scene could be cut together to make it more involving. Intersperse the close-ups and wide shots to add effect.

Don't be afraid to defy convention when you're doing this. Most of the time, a scene opens up with establishing shots before showing the details of what's going on, or close-ups of the characters. Many directors have had great results doing this in the opposite order. James Whale, best known for the Universal *Frankenstein* films from the 1930s, wasn't afraid to open a scene with close-up shots rather than establishing shots of the location.

Make sure you use good film editing theory. Don't use a close-up of an actor and then switch to a slightly different angle. This results in a jarring—and sometimes inadvertently comical—effect.

Be sure you tell the story using different angles. If someone is supposed be terrified in a scene, it's not a bad idea to emphasize this by using angles that constantly make them smaller and smaller, emphasizing the effect.

Be creative. The post-production process is one of the best times to exercise your creativity, so don't waste it.

Keep the Pace
Great movies never stop moving forward. When the dialogue has a lot of necessary but long-winded exposition, the editing oftentimes moves more quickly to keep the audience interested. If someone is explaining something, the editing can make the scene a lot more involving for the audience. For example, if an exposition character is instructing a secret agent on how to use a portable hard drive, the shot might cut to that portable hard drive while the character is speaking. This is a way that editing can keep the scene moving and inform the audience.

The editing process is where you make sure that the film is engaging. It should always be offering the audience something worth listening to or looking at, hopefully, both.

Bad Days Sometimes Produce Good Material
There will be scenes that you'll review in editing that will make you cringe. A bad performance by an actor, a stray boom mic, anything could ruin them; don't toss them out completely.

There may be different angles that you can use in these bad shots. There may also be some good performances among the bad. An actor may have delivered his one monologue that day in a truly brilliant way. Don't throw the baby out with the bathwater in these cases. When you're going to scrap a scene altogether, make sure to note anything that you could potentially use.

Missing Shots
Make notes about the shots that you're missing. When it's all said and done, you're going to have to choose which ones to shoot and which aren't any great loss. A missing shot might make it necessary to scrap an entire scene—or even subplot—but that might be good for the film.

Post-Production

Your pickup shoots are where you'll get all this material that fill in the gaps. If you can schedule your pickup shoots to be done as close together and efficiently as possible, it'll help prevent budget overruns during the post-production process.

Don't Obsess
There is plenty of out there about how audiences will forgive small inconsistencies in editing and it's true. Don't obsess if someone moves across a room and their motion isn't completely natural. For example, if they pick up a coffee cup and move a chair, but the chair isn't quite in the right position in the next cut, the audience will probably not notice, particularly if the character is moving. This is why a lot of editors prefer to make cuts on action.

Don't Get Attached
Take input from the director and the editor seriously. They can help to make sure that the edit makes the film better. If there's a scene or a shot that you love but they think it could go, consider what they have to say. You don't always have to agree, but it's a good idea to be open-minded about this.

Remember that there's probably a director's cut to be made, and that means one more way to market the film!

Time Is Not Real
Does your film move too slowly toward its conclusion? Consider changing the order of the scenes radically. It's very common for movies to be edited together so that the whole thing unfolds backwards or in a convoluted fashion. Some films do this very well; *Memento* is a good example of this.

Consider getting very creative if your film is boring. Sometimes, stories are a lot more interesting if the audience knows what's going to happen first. Don't be afraid to go even further with this. If a scene drags down a film if it's put in the film in order, consider that putting it in earlier or later than originally planned may make it more interesting. A boring exposition becomes an incredible revelation, .

When It's Done
You now have an official rough cut of your film. It isn't anywhere near where it should be, but it's getting there. Watch the rough cut a few times, at least. See what you want to change and make notes. Your director and editor will be doing the same.

About that director's cut; you don't necessarily have to make one and the budget may not allow you to do so. If you do have a director that negotiated the right to make a cut, he or she will do that in coordination with the editor.

If your director wants to make their own cut, remember that it is an effective way to market the movie. It's sometimes more popular with fans than the team cut. *Blade Runner* is an example of a film where both the theatrical and the director's cut got great reviews on their own merits.

Finalize It
After everyone agrees on an edit, you can declare it the final edit. There is one last thing you might want to do to get an idea of whether an alternate editing strategy would be beneficial.

Previewing It

Sometimes, it's a good idea to get viewer input on your film. You can arrange for certain people to watch the rough cut of your film and to offer their opinions on it.

Here's something to keep in mind: Audience input can ruin a film.

Consider a very good film with a realistic or even tragic ending. You might get audience feedback such as "I wish the grandmother hadn't died of cancer." It may be a valid point, but would changing that make it a more satisfying film?

If you utilize a focus group, consider balancing your vision and the point of the story with the input you receive before you make any changes.

Once the final edit is completed, it's time to dress it up. This is where everything starts to come together and the flaws are removed. It's also one of the most exciting times to be a producer. This is where all the blood and sweat you put into the film comes together. The film starts to look like something you'd see in a theater.

Sound

Location sound isn't going to cut it. You will have to record dialogue, add Foley effects, and more to get the right sound.

The sound editing process is both very technical and very aesthetic. The right sound can make a film; bad sound can ruin it. Here's where you have a chance to make your story come to life aurally. Make sure it's done right.

The Process

Films use multi-tracked sound to provide the greatest degree of control over the finished product. This means that every major sound has its own track and that it can be dialed up, dialed down, or completely eliminated without affecting the other sounds. This is why you can always hear people yelling at one another over explosions in movies, even though you probably wouldn't be able to in real life.

The soundtrack will contain some basic elements that are more or less universal. They include the music, the special sound effects, ambient sound used for realism, and dialogue. There may be other tracks added, depending upon the scene. A scene with a voiceover, for example, would have a separate track.

The process takes place under the supervision of the sound editor. Make sure you're working with someone good, because they have a lot of influence over what you'll end up with!

Dialogue

The first step that the sound editor will take is matching the dialogue to the images on the screen. This takes some time.

After this step, you'll see all the problems. This is fixed with ADR, which stands for Automatic Dialogue Replacement. It's also called looping, but it's better to refer to it as ADR, as looping is an entirely different technique that sound editors use .

During ADR, the cast comes into a studio and records their lines. They may end up doing almost the entire script to get consistent audio quality. There are real advantages to this process, so it's worth budgeting sufficient funds to have it done.

Here are some reasons to consider why not skimp on this:

- *Actors like it: It gives them a chance to fine-tune their performances and offer something better,*
- *Control: You're recording under more controlled conditions, which means crisper, clearer dialogue;*
- *One track: Each actor's dialogue gets its own track, which makes it easier to manipulate and edit for the best results;*

- *Better film: Particularly if your film is very dialogue-heavy, do a lot of ADR. If you don't, the audience may not be able to follow the plot as they should.*

Location Sound

The sound mixer will use it to flesh out the picture. It will contain a lot of ambient sounds and other sounds necessary for the film. These sounds can be augmented with Foley sound, which is detailed below.

What Is Foley?

Foley is sound that is added after the movie's location sound has been recorded and added. It emphasizes certain actions on the screen and is as much a part of the narrative as the script and performances.

Foley is not intended to make sounds more realistic. On the contrary, it's added for drama. Many people may assume that a punch sounds like what they hear on screen. In real life, punches are essentially soundless, particularly the ones that do the most damage.

Take a sharp knife, sheath it, and pull it out. Did it make a sound? No, aside from the sound of the steel sliding against the sheath. In a film, it will make a ringing, shimmering sound. This is so common that TV Tropes call it *"Audible Sharpness."* This sound isn't real, but it's great for dramatic effect. It can increase the menace the audience feels when they see the blade or it can make al sword seem magical to the audience.

Foley is incredibly important for the small things. When a character slams down their bottle of beer in rage, it should thump on the bar. When a character takes off in their low-power, front-wheel drive vehicle on a chase, the tires should have a muscle-car squeal. The audience wants this, so give it to them.

Whether it's as subtle as the sound of a door shutting, or as distressing as the sound of bones cracking, Foley makes your movie more interesting, more engaging, and more worth watching.

Who Does It?
Foley artists are respected and knowledgeable individuals with an important job in post-production. This is sometimes their exclusive job on a film. Sometimes they have other roles, such as being the sound editor.

If you're hiring Foley artists from outside, they'll usually have their own studio, or they may show up at yours with an array of different objects. They layer sounds to get the best possible effect. The aforementioned punch, for example, may combine the sounds of someone whipping a car antenna through the air, two steaks being slapped together, and a soft drum hit to get the end result. Every Foley artist has their own way of doing things but, when they are good at it, the results are very impressive.

Sound Effects
Sound effects are usually prerecorded. If someone in your film fires a gun, you don't have to go shoot off hundreds of rounds of ammunition to get the right effect. You can use a special effects library of sounds, such as ".45 ACP, Outdoors, 5 Meters Away." There are sound effects for almost everything: Traffic in New York, traffic in Smalltown, USA, animal sounds, any imaginable weapon firing..

There are e sound effects that have become legendary, such as the Wilhelm Scream. Once it's pointed out, you'll notice that it's in a huge number of films.

The point is, unless the sound has been recycled *ad nauseum*, the audience probably isn't going to notice that a goat in your movie sounds like a goat in another movie. Using libraries is an inexpensive way to get good results and, because of that, any producer should take heed and make sure they use libraries rather than creating custom effects whenever possible.

Sometimes, However

If you're thinking that sound effects are another part of the post-production process, think again. Consider the following:

- *Mad Max's car;*
- *Lightsabers;*
- *Phasers on Star Trek;*
- *The firearms in Saving Private Ryan.*

Sound effects can be distinctive and can become recognizable as part of a story. If you have signature elements in your story—the hero rides a Harley Davidson, —be sure to consider the areas where there is an opportunity to create custom sound effects. Custom sound effects can make a movie stand out, and can contribute to creating a unique universe for the story.

Here's one other thing to consider: If you're shooting a film for between $400,000 and $5,000,000, there may have been compromises that involved deciding not to film scenes that included expensive sequences or special effects.

However, using sound effects and reaction shots, it is possible to realize some of those scenes without ever shooting them. The audience will hear convincing sounds and they will fill in the blanks on their own.

When to Use Either

Technically, Foley sounds are types of sound effects. The difference is that the Foley sounds are created specifically for a scene. This allows the sound to more closely match the scene that the audience is watching. For example, if an actor in your scene pounds on a fencepost with a sledgehammer and the only available stock sound effect is that of somebody pounding a nail into a board, there would be an obvious disconnect, even though the audience might not recognize exactly what it was.

A Foley artist would either get a fencepost and a sledgehammer to re-create the sound directly or create something representative of that sound that has more dramatic effect.

Between blending location sound, replaced dialogue, Foley sounds, and individually crafted special-effects sounds, the entire experience of the film can be greatly enhanced.

There is one other element missing, and that element is vitally important to make certain that the movie has the emotional impact it should. That would be the music. It helps to ensure that the audience feels the emotional impact at the appropriate time.

On a low-budget production, you're not going to be able to afford the biggest names in the film industry to compose your score. Those big-name composers have already done their share of low-budget films on their way to the top, but there are talented musicians waiting to break in.

With the right music, you can vastly change and improve the feeling of a film. You can make it more involving, make it appeal to a specific generation of filmgoers, and more. You can also mix traditional film scoring with individual songs to create an interesting vibe for your film.

Putting Together a Film Score

The person responsible for scoring your film has to know the story inside and out. They need a copy of the script. There are two types of film scoring that you can utilize to great effect, either as the exclusive means of providing the musical background for a film or in combination to add even more of a distinctive feel to your film.

The Traditional Score

A traditional film score is written so that each individual element of the score corresponds to a given scene in the movie. These types of film scores will also have themes for individual characters. For example, Darth Vader is oftentimes announced on screen by the

"Imperial March," one of the most widely known pieces of film music. The character themes certainly can be more subtle.

A traditional film score can give a distinctive feel to a place. Whenever people enter a haunted house on screen, a particular piece of music may start, alerting you that something is about to go awry. This type of film music needs to be composed by somebody with a knowledge of the filmmaking process, and with the technical skills and tools to create a score. For a low-budget picture, it's nearly inconceivable that the production could afford to hire an orchestra to go into a studio and perform each piece of music. Fortunately, that is not a necessity anymore, as will be detailed below.

The Soundtrack Route
The second way a film can be scored is to add existing songs. Oftentimes, this is used along with a film score, and the songs add to the feel of a given scene. For example, when the hero in a movie about bikers gets on their Harley-Davidson to tear down the highway, 1960s or 1970s rock music might start blaring, adding a bit of flavor to the scene. There are a lot of classic films that have used this to great effect. Stanley Kubrick, Quentin Tarantino, and many other directors have done very well by including pieces of music—classical or pop—that exist outside of the film within their films.

Rights
Here's the tricky part about using music that wasn't specifically written for a film. You have to secure the rights to use it in a film. ASCAP handles selling licenses for music and you need to purchase two different types of licenses to use a song in a movie. You first have to get the Synchronization License, which allows you to take a piece of music and to sync it up to the movie that you have created. The second license is called a Master Use License, and this gives you the right to have that music reproduced in your film.

Even though this sounds like a rather complicated process, it is something that can easily be taken care of during the final stages of post-production. There will be cases when an artist or a record label will not allow a certain piece of music to be used in a film. This is usually no great loss. Something else can be found that fits the bill perfectly.

One thing to be very careful of: don't confuse public domain music with public domain performances. Beethoven's Fifth Symphony is in the public domain. Particular performances of Beethoven's Fifth Symphony may be owned by the orchestra that performed them, the record label that distributed it, and so forth. Make certain you look into the rights status of any piece of music before you use it.

Remember that up-and-coming artists will sometimes be willing to put their music in a film for next to nothing. It's a huge opportunity for them and they know it. If you hear a particularly good but relatively unknown band performing somewhere, and you have an instinct that what they are playing would fit perfectly in your film, be sure to talk to them. You might be able to save your production quite a bit of money and help out a musician looking for a break at the same time.

Electronic Scoring
Because of the reduced cost and the great deal of flexibility it affords, many of the people who score films and certainly many producers find that electronic scoring is preferable to having musicians play compositions live. Electronic music, and the instruments available to create it, have come a long way in past decades. While anything less than a top-notch composer with very expensive gear would have resulted in a cheesy, cheap-sounding score in the past, today's electronic instruments are advanced enough that they can be as beautiful and complex as any orchestra.

A composer with modest equipment and a good working knowledge of how to use it can create masterful scores. These scores can be remarkably effective as orchestral enhancements to a film. Best of all, it's far less likely to break the budget. Electronic instruments do not make mistakes, meaning no retakes and other error-related expenses.

Popular Options for Film Scoring

If you hire a composer who has a great deal of experience, they'll likely have the necessary software. What they use will depend on whether they use a Mac or a PC, but this won't be relevant to anyone except for the composer. Some of the popular options for scoring films include:

- *Finale;*
- *Acid Pro;*
- *Cubase;*
- *Sonic;*
- *Logic Pro.*

These programs streamline the composition process in various ways. Finale, allows the composer to create sheet music, which can be used by musicians or for reference during the synching process. Acid Pro allows the musician to lay down separate tracks and edit them.

No matter what type of software they use, it's much more likely that a low-budget film will be able to keep within its budget if the film is scored electronically.

If you are concerned that using an electronic score will cheapen the film, keep in mind that some of the most popular and praised soundtracks have been done electronically. The question is not whether or not electronic instruments can offer acceptable results. The question is whether you want the score to sound like a live orchestra—which is doable—or if you want to capitalize on what electronic instruments have to offer in their own right. Some films to look at—or listen to—that make very good use of electronic instruments include:

- *Drive*: 2011
- The Terminator: 1984
- *Dune*: 1984
- Blade Runner: 1982
- The Social Network: 2010

- *Tron*: 2010

Note that some of these were big-budget films. Using electronic instruments for the score, when it's done properly, is certainly not a compromise. If the scoring is particularly good, the music might stand out to audiences as one of the best things about the film.

The Scoring Process
The composer should be scheduled to come in around the time that the rough cut is finished. Bring them in earlier only if you want them to capture a particular feeling for a scene or if you want them to be exposed to an actor's performance in person. There is usually no need for this.

Setting the Mood
Schedule some time to meet with the composer and to go over what you're looking for with them. The director should be a part of this, at least, but consider including other key production staff.

The cinematography and the score can work hand-in-hand to create a mood that pulls the audience into the film. In the 2013 film, *Man of Steel*, flashbacks to the character's youth are oftentimes shown in a filtered light with a sparse piano line that lends them a very surreal—even sad—quality. In the aforementioned *Dune*, Brian Eno's soundtrack is characteristically ambient and droning, lending to the sense of emptiness and the surreal quality of many of the desert shots and the visions that the protagonist experiences.

Tell the Story, or Add to It
Remember to keep in mind that you can add subtleties to the soundtrack that, if the film gets a strong fan base, can serve as Easter eggs for them to find. In the film *Hellraiser 2*, the soundtrack plays out the Morse code for G-O-D when the entity Leviathan is depicted on the screen.

Inception features a lot of subtle clues and meanings in the soundtrack . There are plenty of films that have used the soundtrack to tell the story, to some degree, or to enhance elements of it so that the audience is more involved in what unfolds on the screen.

Character Themes

Important characters oftentimes have themes associated with them. Go over these characters in detail with the person writing the score, as the right theme can make a character more memorable. Most hero characters will have a hero theme. A great example of this is the triumphant march that plays every time Indiana Jones does anything heroic on-screen in the series of films featuring that character.

Some Vocabulary

Because filmmaking is such a visual process, some of the top people in the production—including the producer—are likely to have a vocabulary that's more appropriate for describing the visual elements of a film. Where music is concerned, here are some vocabulary terms that can help a producer to get the idea across to a composer, possibly eliminating some frustration:

Classical: Classical is technically a form of music associated with a specific era, but the term can be used to communicate that something traditional and orchestral is called for.

Industrial: Industrial music relies on synthesizers, distortion and a lot of ambience, along with other diverse elements. *The Social Network* is a good example of a film that uses elements of this style.

Rave Music: This can be used to loosely refer to any driving, electronic music that is obviously made for dancing. There are innumerable variations on this, but most of it is characterized by a driving 4/4 beat and loud, simple synthesizer scenes. It's a staple of film party scenes.

Dubstep: A modern form of electronic music that is characterized by a rather daring use of frequencies, particularly at the very low end.

Folky or Folk: Indie movies use this type of music frequently. Think one man or woman and a guitar, or a alt-country feel if you want to imply that the character is a bit rebellious.

Music Montages

Using a set of scenes cut to music is a great way to tell a story. It's also a great way to cut down on the number of scenes that shoot for a film. This technique is used to show the passage of time or to simply spare the audience having to sit through scene after scene of exposition. When it's done right, a few minutes of musical montage can take the place of many exposition scenes that might leave the audience yawning.

This is one area where, if you're using actual songs written by a band, consider inserting them into the soundtrack. There are many examples of this technique in films. Television shows use it to cram several episodes of drama into a couple of minutes of expositional visual sequences. *Sons of Anarchy*, on the FX network, has gotten praise for its use of music montages.

Keep in mind that putting a song with a theme that clashes with what's transpiring on screen can be very effective in an ironic sort of way. The aforementioned television show used "What a Wonderful World" for a montage that featured very violent content.

Score vs. Soundtrack

There are some subtleties in how people differentiate between a soundtrack and a score. Essentially the distinction is an easy one to make.

When someone composes music that is designed to sync to a part of a film, it is a score. A soundtrack may contain such pieces, but it can also contain music that plays in the film and that was not composed specifically for the film.

There are oftentimes two separate albums released as ways to bring up the profits from a film. The soundtrack will contain all songs used in the film that exist outside of the film. For example, if you used a song from an indie band in a film about college students, that song would appear on the soundtrack. The original score for the film usually appears on a separate album.

Syncing
The composer will review the rough edit with the producer, the director and anyone else involved. The people involved in the creative process will start deciding where music needs to be added and the composer will note at which time in the movie that every piece of music is intended to be played on the soundtrack. The score might include names for the pieces such as these:

- *The House Theme 1:30;*
- *A Ghost in the Dark 2:34;*
- *Fall from the Window 2:50.*

The soundtrack and score elements can be synched by the sound department after they are mixed and ready to go.

Remember to get creative with this. In the 1979 film *Alien*, , the filmmakers played with audience expectations by not cluing them into the presence of the antagonist by foregoing a distinctive theme every time it was lurking in the darkness of the ship. On the other hand, when the shark in *Jaws* was in the water, the audience certainly knew about it, courtesy of the distinctive and memorable shark theme.

The score will be, if it is done right, a major part of the film experience. If you cannot afford an established composer to handle the scoring duties, look for a talented amateur and encourage them to be creative. Sometimes, a bad score can make a low-budget film come off as even lower-budget than it is, so be sure to invest some creativity into this process, even if the budget prevents investing a lot of dollars into it.

Special Effects

Where special effects are concerned, there are three broad types that you have to concern yourself with.

Optical Effects: These are done in-camera and are handled during shooting. The quality of these effects is dependent on the skill of your camera operators, DP, director, and everyone else involved in the actual shoot.

Mechanical Effects: These are oftentimes referred to as practical effects. At their best, they include animatronics, miniatures and other elements that are used to create convincing effects that ramp up the storytelling. At their worst, they include the cheesy rubber monsters that were so popular in '50s and '60s sci-fi and horror.

CGI: This stands for Computer Generated Imagery and is quickly becoming the dominant type of special effect. It can be combined with the other two types to make them more convincing, or it can be used on its own to create some marvelous effects. CGI is expensive, so it's usually reserved for films with a larger budget.

This section will look at how these effects are used to create involving movie experiences as well as how they can make low-budget films look truly awful.

Optical Effects
One of the limitations of film is that it is two-dimensional. That can be turned into an asset with the right equipment and the right people.

For example, one of the most popular ways to crate imaginative—and sometimes impossible—locations is to use a matte painting. This is a large painting of a landscape that the actors stand in front of, giving the impression that they are standing anywhere the action calls for them to be. The original three *Star Wars* films used this to great effect.

In *The Lord of the Rings* trilogy, one of the most impressive uses of optical effects in modern filmmaking is on bold display. The scenes where the hobbits appear were not CGI. In these scenes, tricks of perspective were used to make the hobbit characters appear smaller than everyone else. This resulted in, what most would agree, a very convincing film.

There's something to keep in mind about these sorts of effects: They can be very expensive. Having a matte painting produced may involve many hours of labor and a lot of materials, if you want it to look good. Optical effects, such as the forced perspective used in *The Lord of the Rings* trilogy, require that special sets and props be built, which is labor intensive and also eats time.

Never mind the fact that your camera people and director need to be up to this challenge, which is considerable. If you have a good crew, you could get everything you needed for the optical effects during the regular shooting schedule. More likely you'll be looking at pickup shoots, very expensive ones at that.

FX shots should be called out in your shooting schedule. The director and AD will generally go through the process with you, letting you know if they need accommodations for shooting in-camera effects on any given day of shooting.

One alternative to using matte paintings is to use a blue or green screen and insert a computer-generated background into the picture during post-production. This will be covered in the upcoming section on CGI.

Mechanical Effects

Mechanical effects are staples of filmmaking. Like any other type of effect, they are called for in the shooting script and the shooting schedule, so these will have been arranged and shot by the time you get to post-production. You can use editing, music, and other resources to up their effectiveness.

The people who put together mechanical effects are part artist, part engineer, and part mad scientist. The right people can build creatures that can make the audience jump or squirm, create body effects that can be stirring and inspiring—the hero shoots claws from out of their hand, *a la* Wolverine, for example—or that are revolting, such as the famous chest-buster scene from the original *Alien*.

Like Foley artists, mechanical effects wizards oftentimes employ odd materials to create the effect that you need. They might have to create android blood and innards, such as in *Alien*, or something far simpler, such as making the nightmare-inducing clown doll in *Poltergeist* lunge out at one of the protagonists. Either way, mechanical effects can be, and oftentimes are, more convincing than their computer-generated substitutes.

Some examples of mechanical effects include:

- *Wire fighting (when characters engage in impossible fighting moves while suspended by wires);*
- *Gunshots, knife stabs, sword wounds, etc.*
- *Explosions and fires;*
- *Rain and snow;*
- *Dummies used in place of actors for stunts that are too dangerous to do in person;*
- *Monsters;*
- *Vehicles such as space ships and ocean ships;*
- *Miniature sets.*

These effects are sometimes accomplished with devices that are designed to perform a series of automated actions and are sometimes animated by shooting them frame-by-frame. The starship battles in *Star Wars*—at least the first three movies—were oftentimes shot frame-by-frame. The fighters and other ships ending up appearing to move in the film. In other cases, such as the aforementioned chest-burster scene in the original *Alien* films, the Walkers in EMPIRE STRIKES BACK were done using stop motion animation combined with green or blue screen shots.

During the shooting of the Alien scene, incidentally, the effects were so convincing and unexpected that one of the actresses passed out and they all agreed that it was far more intense than they expected. Never underestimate the effectiveness of a well-executed practical effect. They can be far more memorable than a CGI effect. When these effects are done right, they have the advantage of being real. Rather than the actors reacting to something that they're supposed to imagine and having that scenario created by computers after the effect, the film shows something that happened live on camera and that the actors reacted to with genuine, and appropriate, emotions.

Hazards

Mechanical effects can be dangerous, even deadly. Sometimes, the danger comes not from elaborate mechanical contraptions that could pose a risk, but from everyday objects in the world of film.

Brandon Lee, son of Bruce Lee, met an untimely death while acting on the set of *The Crow*. The scene he died in was standard movie fare: The hero enters a room and is gunned down by an antagonist character. The gun that was used for the scene was loaded with a blank, but it still contained a piece of a prop bullet that had been used earlier in the shoot. When the actor playing the antagonist shot Lee, the blank pushed the prop bullet down the barrel, killing Lee.

Whenever mechanical effects are being used, it's vital to have a safety supervisor involved to make sure that that no one is being put in harm's way.

Stunt people are specially trained to deal with dangerous situations on sets. If you're worried about the safety of an effects sequence and want to make sure that your actors—not having that training—aren't at serious risk, have a qualified stunt person perform the stunt. Proper equipment and setup can prevent a tragedy or even save a life.

Special attention has to be given to guns, blades, chemicals, fire and explosives, and all of those things require specialized training to handle.

It's also imperative that proper permitting is obtained to ensure that the shoot doesn't cross legal boundaries or put anyone or anyone's property at risk. Additionally, for location shoots, notices should be posted. The last thing a producer needs is the police showing up on a set because a neighbor heard gunshots and screaming.

Mechanical effects can be difficult to budget unless you know how they're to be created. This is best done with the assistance of the effects people themselves and done well in advance of shooting.

CGI

CGI has made the impossible possible for filmmakers. It's also led to some very bad film special effects and, for some fans, it's never convincing. When it's done right, it can be used to create beautiful landscapes and incredible battles. When it's done poorly—or on the cheap—it produces results that are comparable to a badly animated video game. Because this will to be used heavily on a low-budget film, it bears some examination.

What Is It?

CGI is a catchall term for any image added to a film that is created in a computer during the post-production process. Accommodations for this are usually made during the shoot. In many films where a character is talking to a monster of some sort, they're talking to a tennis ball on a stick. The color of the tennis ball is distinctive enough that it is easy to isolate and remove from the frame in post-production. It will be replaced with a dragon, a robot, or whatever else is needed.

CGI can be subtle or intense. It can be something as simple as adding the flames to candles that couldn't be lit during a shoot because of safety reasons. It can be as complex—or, some would say, distracting—as Jar Jar Binks, the rather controversial character from *The Phantom Menace* and other *Star Wars* prequel films.

The thing to remember with CGI, particularly where films with lower budgets are concerned, is that more is not necessarily better.

Moderation in All Things

The more CGI is on the screen, the more noticeable it will be and that means that the illusion will not stand up. A magician, after all, never reveals how they're doing their tricks and, if the audience saw how it was done, they'd never be involved in the illusion again. This is important to keep in mind where CGI is concerned.

Some examples of CGI gone wrong that have done so in otherwise very well received films. In *I Am Legend*, for example, What Culture points out that one of the climatic scenes features a monster that, because it is CGI, doesn't have the screen presence it should. Here are some of the common pitfalls of using CGI too gratuitously:

- *CGI-created living creatures tend to have unnatural movement, particularly facial movements;*
- *It is nearly impossible to recreate the look of a living being's eyes;*
- *CGI landscapes can appear flat and unconvincing;*
- *The physics of CGI are sometimes giveaways that the scene or creature is not real.*

Where CGI is concerned, the artists can do remarkable things, given the proper budget. On a lower-budget film it may be better to go with practical effects or to use even simpler effects that don't require anything sophisticated at all.

As an example of how effective that latter method can be, consider the 2005 version of *War of the Worlds*. In that film, there is a scene where the protagonists are hiding in a basement. Some event is happening outside. The entire scene is told with lighting flashing through the window, sound, and the reactions of the actors. In the end, we see that what transpired was a plane crash. Without any CGI airplane crashing into the ground, Spielberg managed to create an engaging scene that told the entire story.

Sometimes, even when your budget is essentially whatever you want it to be, simpler, less effects-driven storytelling methods work better. With good actors, it's possible to engage an audience in a way that effects can't rival.

Green and Blue Screens

If you've ever stood in front of a green screen or a blue screen, you've probably cringed a bit. The colors are unnatural and harsh and that's exactly the idea. Using a technique called chroma key, the entire green screen or blue screen in the shot can be removed in post-production and replaced with whatever the animators need to conjure up. This is a very old technique and, for most low-budget films that have any kind of exotic location requirements, it's going to be a necessity. It can be very affordable; certainly more affordable than taking the whole crew to White Sands to get a dream or alien world sequence.

TIP: Remember that the green or blue screen cannot blend with the colors of props and costume. If you're shooting a movie with a SWAT team , you wouldn't want to use a blue screen, as the color would blend too much with the police uniforms.

The Actor's Perspective

Whenever you shoot a green or blue screen scene, you change something very important for the actors in the scene. Rather than interacting with the environment, they're standing in front of a flat screen pretending that they're somewhere else. It's even more involved for the actor if they have to react to something that's going to be placed into the scene during post-production, such as one of the aforementioned movie monsters. Here are some ways that you can make this easier on the actor.

First, if there is something or someone to which they are supposed to react, have another actor work with the main actor or actors in the scene. You can use a suit the same color as the screen so that this person can be removed from the final edit of the scene altogether. This is a great way to get the actor to behave more naturally. It's particularly important if the actor is supposed to have direct physical contact with whatever's going to be put into the scene in postproduction.

Second, make sure the actor knows what the location is supposed to look like. For example, people in magnificent cathedrals oftentimes look up at the ceiling and the actor may want to add that to their performance. It can make the FX scenery seem more real for the audience. Likewise, if they're in a hot desert and a wind is blowing their cloak around, it's a lot easier to give a good performance if the actor is aware of the landscape than it is if they know that they're in front of a green screen with a fan blowing at them.

Where these effects are concerned, a good deal of how convincing they are will come down to how well the actor portrays their character in the situation.

With Matte Paintings

If you watch some older films, it's obvious that the actors are standing in front of a painting. Newer films tend to combine the painting with the chroma key technique.

One money-saving way to accomplish this is to take stills of the locations that you want in the film. Insert these shots into the blue or green screen image during post-production. This results in a very natural-looking background, as the lighting and other elements will look realistic. This can make the effect a lot more interesting.

When to Cut Effects

Special-effects shots can be very expensive. If they take a lot of work and equipment, they can easily drive a film over budget.

There will be times when you, as the producer, have to make an executive decision and cut scenes where the effects cost too much. Sadly, you may not have this realization until a lot of work has already been done on a given scene. In such cases, it's important to not let good money follow bad. If it's not working, cut it rather than blowing your entire budget on finishing a scene that's not working. Failing to cut your losses endangers the quality of the rest of the film.

Here are some things to consider if a given FX scene is pushing a low-budget film over the brink:

Is the Scene Necessary?

Does it drive the plot forward? Does it help to show the characters developing in some way? If not, it might be something that the film can do without. Remember that audiences are accustomed to over-the-top effects these days, so having some special effects in the film is not necessarily going to wow them in any meaningful way.

Are the Effects Too Much?

Do you need 200 ships in the space battle or could you get away with 10? Do you need 15 goons firing automatic weapons or could you show the actor reacting to getting shot at and get the same result?

Is It Necessary for Perspective?

If you have a good actor, they can eliminate the need for special effects by giving a good emotional performance. Imagine someone abandoning an aircraft carrier that's under attack; you don't necessarily have to show an aircraft carrier in flames. If your actor is good, you might be able to create the same tension with a good performance, tracking shots, great lighting, and a few explosions here and there. Be creative and you might be able film a big scene and stay in budget.

The Tough Cuts

As the producer, you have to make some hard calls about cutting scenes. These may be scenes that the director and others want to keep in the film. Some of this was previously covered from an artistic standpoint, but there are other reasons that you may have to cut scenes from a film. Consider the following examples:

Ratings

Part of the job of a producer is to balance the artistic vision of the film with the necessity that the film has to be profitable. Ratings play a major part in how successful a film can be.

Film ratings are set by the MPAA, the Motion Picture Association of America. Most major releases are rated R or less. NC-17 can be a death sentence where profitability is concerned.

G: General Audiences. This means that the film is appropriate for anyone of any age. In practice, it means that the film is intended for young children.

PG: Parental Guidance Suggested. This rating means that the film might contain some material that's a bit too much for young children. In practice, it still means "kids' movie."

PG-13: This raises the bar a little bit from PG where content is concerned. It means, essentially, that the film contains material that might be too shocking or frightening for younger children, but most teenagers will be okay with it. This came about in the '80s; more on that below.

R: Restricted. This means that a parent must go to the movie with their child if that child is under 17. While this rating does cut out the teen market somewhat, most serious dramas, realistic action films, and certainly most horror films are given this rating.

NC-17: No Children Under 17. This is basically what used to be called an "X" rating. These films are intended for adults only.

Unrated: In a world where DVDs and online play are as important as theater play to some films, this is certainly an option. Films that are unrated have never been submitted for a viewing and a subsequent rating.

Marketability and Compromises
In 1984, Lucasfilm released the first sequel to the Spielberg blockbuster *Raiders of the Lost Ark. Indiana Jones and the Temple of Doom* surprised some parents. Scenes where people had their hearts ripped out of their chests and other intense violence caused some controversy. Spielberg used his influence to help create the PG-13 rating. The idea was simple; a human sacrifice scene will

terrify a young child, but a teenager would see it as intense, if violent, entertainment.

PG-13 is one of the most sought-after ratings in Hollywood for a simple reason. It opens up the film to the very lucrative teenage market without having to water the film down enough to get a PG rating.

Whether it's cynicism—all those teenagers, all that money—or genuine concern—all those parents having to get a terrified child to bed after a movie scarier than they expected—the rating has worked out very well. For some low-budget film projects, getting a rating of PG-13 could open up entirely new markets for the material. Then again, it could also ruin the film.

Getting a Rating

Artists have long suffered under the yoke of organizations that want to make sure that nothing offends anyone, anywhere, ever. The MPAA is sometimes seen in this light. The organization uses an independent panel of parents to determine which rating a film should receive.

Unless no one bothered to read the script, most producers will know where they're headed when they start shooting a film. An intense thriller about drug dealers on the run will definitely get an R rating. That means teenagers won't be able to see it in the theater, but it also makes the film more attractive to adults, even though that's not the intention of ratings.

Movie ratings have gotten a bit suspect in terms of the sly marketing they enable the studio to do. PG-13 might be sub-rated with a warning such as "Intense Sci-Fi Action." If one were to put an exclamation point after that, it would practically be a sales brochure.

Disturbing images, sexual situations, partial nudity, etc., are all things that show up in ratings. If you want to get to an R from an

NC-17 or to shift to PG-13 from an R, you might have to do some cutting.

If your film comes back with a rating higher than you want, you might find yourself in a tricky situation. The movie might qualify for a PG-13 rating if there is nudity, but it is not sexual. There are a lot of vagaries in this. On the MPAA site, it notes that "harsher sexually-derived words" may influence whether or not a PG-13 rating can be obtained. What defines "harsher" words is very subjective. Such is the ratings system.

Cutting to Get a Rating

Sometimes, you'll be able to cut certain scenes that bring the rating to a less restrictive one without much influence on the vision of the film. Other times, not so much. If someone had cut *Saw* to a PG-13 film, it would have been about 20 minutes long. On the other hand, some films manage to get away with lowering their rating by cutting out one or two gory sequences, or a few profanity-laced tirades and remain essentially the same film. The decision is up to the producer and the other higher-ups in the production process. That decision is based on money as much as art.

Unrated

The ratings system is designed to make things easier for parents. What if you're not worried about parents who have to supervise their children because your film was never intended for children in the first place? Some low-budget films go straight to DVD and online viewing. What then?

Sometimes, in these cases, you may be able to skip the ratings process altogether or, alternately, to release an unrated version that is suited to the vision that drove the film.

The unrated version is not the same as the director's cut, though the director's cut may contain some of the scenes that were removed out of sensitivity to the MPAA system. The unrated version is a version of a film that was cut together in a way that best suited the artistic vision or that, quite simply, gave the fans what they wanted. This is a very popular way to release movies after their theatrical run, which will be covered in the next section, Dealing with Distribution.

The unrated versions of films are sometimes more popular with fans and end up becoming the preferred versions of those films. Some viewers believe the fact that the studios have to stay within the bounds of an R rating for commercial viability smacks of censorship and stifles artistic creativity. Whether or not this is the case depends upon the movie you're making.

On the positive side, it enables you to release two different versions of the movie. There's a good chance that people will be interested in seeing an unrated version of a film that they liked in its MPAA-approved incarnation. There's also a hazard here.

Sometimes, making accommodations for a better rating can make a film better. The gore may be more effective when it's implied rather than seen, particularly if the effects are lacking. The language might be better if a few F-bombs are cut, allowing the audience to concentrate on what is being said rather than the profanity.

This gets into the final three elements of the post-production process. Success or failure in this area will depend upon how well the producer, director, and others have done up until this point.

Preserving Vision
When a movie production starts, it's because of a vision. There was a script or novel that told a compelling story. The producer believed in it enough to do the hard work of getting it funded. The director brought it to life. The cast and crew put blood, sweat, and tears into making it a reality. That vision matters.

Throughout the production process, there will be many voices telling the producer and others that compromise is needed. Sometimes this is true, but think about what might be lost if filmmakers had been too eager to compromise.

What if Quentin Tarantino had decided *Pulp Fiction* was too violent and offensive and had dialed it down a bit? Would it have been the same movie? What if Rose, at the end of *Titanic*, had pointed out that there was plenty of extra room on the wreckage she was floating on for her poor lover Jack—there was—and they had both been rescued? Would the film have been nearly as engaging?

Probably not, in either case, and in many others where the producer and director stood behind what they'd created, no matter how much more family-friendly—or at least less depressing—their films would have been if they'd compromised.

There is something to be said for preserving vision, and as a producer, you will be have to fight for it. Sometimes, it's definitely worth the battle. But, sometimes, it's not.

Improving Vision
Sometimes, a bit of input can be helpful. Cutting a few scenes here and there might be painful, but it might be for the best.

When directors and producers become too involved in their films, they can get a bit out-of-hand, forgetting that the story may be compelling to them, but not be as interesting to the audience. One good example of this is the *Star Wars* prequels. In the prequels, the stories involve long-winded dissertations on treaties, politics, and even taxes. The scenes are much more crowded. In the original trilogy, the scenes and dialogs were simple and much less crowded. On the surface of it, it would seem that the prequels are more ornate, complex, and cerebral, but they have gotten widespread criticism for slow pacing and, essentially, being boring and overdone.

A director and a producer may have a great vision, but it may need to be cut back before it's something memorable. If someone's input implies that cutting certain elements will make the initial vision work, consider that they may be right.

Commercial Viability: It Matters

The film has been completed. It is ready to be distributed and, in every sense, is a complete package.

The commercial viability of this film, and what you put into making sure it was commercially viable, will come into play. If you made a great art film, you might be able to get it shown at film festivals, but it is less likely to get onto a commercial theater's screen.

How well your film will perform commercially matters. It will affect how many projects you'll helm in the future, and will influence who wants to work with you on those films. It will influence how readily funders will come through with money when you need it.

Before you get prickly about oppression from the studios or sacrificing vision for commercial concerns, remember that films are supposed to be things that people want to watch. If you want to make films for your art-genius friends to watch, you can do that, but no one will pony up the money to pay for it.

When reviewing the finished package, put some time into consider if you have a blockbuster. Have it test-screened to see what audiences like and take their feedback seriously, even if you don't cut the film based on it. Look at your finished project and ask yourself if it's good.

There is a cottage industry of Internet film critics out there. Some of them have very little to say and say it anyway. Some of them are very good at critique and are worth hearing out. When you're reviewing that final cut of the film, look at criticism of similar films in the same genre and see if you're repeating other people's mistakes. If you are, reconsider some of your decisions.

Then again, you may not want to reconsider them. Part of the work of being a producer is making the toughest decisions in the movie business.

When it is finished and ready to go, you'll have to work out distribution and marketing for the film. This is a huge undertaking in and of itself. On low-budget films, you may be doing this without the support of a studio or the funders. You'll have to be on top of things and understand how this business works to get your film distributed and seen. The next chapters will address these challenges.

Chapter 7

Distribution

All of the work a producer puts into making a great film is worthless if no one sees it. Distribution is about getting the film into theaters and onto store shelves. Distribution is sometimes set up for the film right away, but there are plenty of cases where the producer will have to work to find the right distributor; one willing to make a deal that allows the producer and other involved parties to make a tidy profit off the film.

Distribution depends upon some of the variables that have been discussed already; if you were unwilling to cut the film to avoid an NC-17 rating, you can kiss goodbye any chances of getting that film distributed in regular theaters. If you managed to score an R or PG-13 rating, you'll find that the theaters of the world are open for your film, but that you still need to do the hard work of getting it out there, and all the wheeling and dealing that goes along with that.

Why Bother?

Before getting into how to find a distributor, it's important to understand why a distributor is of such benefit for a film. After all, the world is full of options for people who want to distribute their own work. The Internet is full of ways that people can self-distribute anything, from major shopping sites, to sites that specialize in independent film. There are even streaming stations that allow you to have your movie broadcast, as it were.

For a low-budget film, the only real route to success is through the distributor. The distributor will take a chunk of your profits, but they can also make sure that your film has the best chance of success. Let's look at some of the ways that a film distributor can make that happen:

Theaters Still Matter, a Lot

Theaters are still vital to the success of any film. There are multiple reasons why this is the case, aside from the obvious fact that theater seats can be very profitable.

Promotion

Promoting a movie costs money. Sometimes it costs a lot of money. At minimum, you will incur the following expenses during your promotion efforts:

Press releases: These are sent to the media to inform them about the film, usually nationwide. This means that it costs money. If you have studio support, they will have a network set up for this.

Advertising: Television, the Internet, newspaper, and magazines are all viable advertising media for films. Television trailers can greatly increase the public interest in a film. Some trailers are as memorable as the films that they advertised.

Film festivals: Getting play at film festivals, covered later in this chapter, can be an important source of publicity for low-budget films, particularly if they fit in a genre for which there is a specific festival. Film festivals involve a lot of travelling, promotion, and general schmoozing.

Pre-screenings: You'll have to set up pre-screenings of the film. Even though these aren't designed to bring in money directly, they're necessary to get the theaters interested in showing your film. Again, this costs money and, sometimes, quite a bit of it, depending on how you set it up.

All these efforts require an investment and the investors want to make sure they have the best possible chance of making their money back. As the producer, it's your duty to make sure that the films you produce are as profitable as possible. More than anything, it means that the film needs a viable chance of earning that money back, and then some.

Distribution Models

When you have a film to promote, there will be any number of people and businesses out there who will be happy to do the work for you, for a fee. Sometimes, these fees are the equivalent of burning money. This isn't always because you're dealing with somebody who is running some sort of a scam. In some cases, the models of distribution promised by more modern film distributors can offer what they promised, but the deals don't turn out to be that good for the people involved in making the film.

There is a very traditional model for film distribution that most low-budget pictures will likely benefit from. There are also models of distribution that are much newer than the traditional model and that might promise a bit more than they deliver in terms of how much money the filmmakers stand to get from utilizing these types of distribution models.

To start with, we will look at the traditional method of film distribution and how you might be able to employ it to turn your low-budget film into a very profitable investment.

The Traditional Distribution Model

Two basic models are utilized in the film industry for film distribution. They are the leasing model and the profit-sharing model. They work much differently, so it's important to understand each of them and, further, to understand which model would be more suitable for the film that you want to distribute.

If a low-budget film you produced happened to be produced with the backing of a major studio, the distribution for the film may already be set up. Some of the larger studios have their own distributors, which makes it much easier to negotiate distribution deals and to deal with profits and losses. Because many low-budget films are likely to be funded by very small studios that may not have such a setup and because some low-budget film producers will have to handle distribution on their own, it's useful to understand these two models and which one of them may be more suitable for the film.

Leasing
Leasing is an arrangement that allows the distributor to lease the rights to distribute the film. As the filmmaker, you make money off this lease, which is negotiated to last for a specified amount of time.

The lease may include the right to distribute the film in theaters, but it may also include the right to distribute the film via DVD, over the Internet on streaming sites, and on television. If the distribution deal is comprehensive, the distribution company may even get the right to distribute merchandise associated with the film, which can be very profitable. For an idea of how profitable merchandise related to a film can be, all one needs to do is look at the *Star Wars* franchise.

Profit Sharing
Profit sharing is a distribution model that involves the distributor getting a cut of any profits that the film generates. The amount of money that the distributor takes can be quite substantial. In some cases, the distributor may end up taking a full 50% of the net profits generated by the film, which obviously cuts into the profits available for everybody else involved in the production substantially.

Under either model, it's important that the distribution company has the resources to distribute and promote the film in a way that will to generate a profit. The distribution company will look at some of the characteristics of the film to determine whether they think they can make a profit distributing it. If they don't feel that they can, they may want more money from profit sharing. or they may want to pay less in a lease to make up for the fact that they don't believe that the movie will perform particularly well.

Things to Keep in Mind Moving Forward

Not all filmmakers choose the typical distribution model for films. Some filmmakers, particularly independent filmmakers, are looking for ways to distribute their films on their own. to avoid what they consider wastes of investment that will be required by distributors, ultimately cutting into the profits that the film could generate.

It's easy to provide an example of what irks some filmmakers about how films are typically distributed. In a *New York Times* story, an independent filmmaker makes a claim that newspaper ads are "mostly a waste of money." There is some truth to this. Newspapers have been struggling to retain readership and, at the same time, it's not particularly more affordable to advertise in newspapers than it was in the past. Distribution companies will generally want to place a lot of advertisements in newspapers for a film, though many independent filmmakers believe that this is not necessarily worthwhile.

In the above-referenced article and in other sources, it's common to see ideas espoused such as that social media has made advertising in traditional venues obsolete. The thing to keep in mind is that the jury is still out on the value of advertising on social media sites and in many other web venues. While it may seem like a cost-effective—even basically free—method of promoting a film, it does lack the prestige of advertising the film in traditional venues.

Think of it this way. There are, quite literally, nearly 1,000,000,000 people on the largest social media site—Facebook—and many others using social media on other sites. These people are constantly bombarded by a flood of advertising and, for the most part, it doesn't necessarily seem that they're paying attention to it.

The traditional venues for advertising films may be a bit less technologically glamorous than some of the other options, but forgoing them altogether to save a few bucks on distribution may not be worth it. This is something that a producer has to discuss with the studio backing the film, other investors and any other parties that have a direct interest in the profits generated by the film.

A Good Point

One of the options that is worth considering as far as distribution goes—particularly if you are interested in avoiding the costs associated with traditional distribution—is hiring a consultant. The consultant will provide much of the same advice as a distribution company would, which is detailed below. The difference is that the consultant typically does not take anywhere near as large a cut of the profits as a distribution company would. This allows the filmmakers to make more of a profit.

While there are more movies being made than ever before, the Hollywood system isn't set up to support many of these films. Many low-budget and independent films—oftentimes low-budget films end up being independent films—are promoted by people who either cannot find a traditional distributor to handle their film or who want to avoid the system altogether.

Using the consultant model, it is possible to get a film shown in theaters, though the release will usually be far more limited than it would if the film were released through traditional channels. That being said, because consultants don't take such a large cut of the profits, it's possible for an independent filmmaker to get their films shown in theaters, make a profit off it and, in some cases, to enjoy quite a bit of success.

Which method a producer wants to follow is entirely up to them and the other people involved in the production and distribution of the film. There are more options out there than there have ever been before and some of those options may be better choices for low-budget films that don't have much of a chance of capturing the interest of major distributors.

Getting Your Materials Ready

Perhaps the one big advantage of finding a distribution deal versus finding funding for a new film project is the fact that you are starting out with a completed product. You don't have to pitch the film so much anymore, as you can show it to people.

In order to get a distributor interested in your film, you have to send them what is called a DVD screener. This is the main part of a promotional package that you will be send them to get them interested in your film. To make things even more complicated, you will be generally be working through a representative, usually called a sales agent. The sales agent is essentially a broker that works out the deal between you and the distributor. In order to do that, the sales agent will need a good package to work with.

The promotion of the film starts even before it hits the theaters. You will be want the following materials to give to distributors through your sales agent:

- *A poster for the film;*
- *Promotional brochures for the film;*
- *Photos taken on the set;*
- *A DVD screener.*

All of these materials can be combined together in a package. The idea is to create something that entices the distributor to look at the film, which happens during a screening. This is where the DVD screener comes into play. Because we are living in the digital age, it is vitally important that a producer understands some real hazards that go along with a DVD screener.

Screener Hazards
If you want to look at the world you're dealing with today, all you have to do is visit some of the websites that are rather notorious for

pirating movies. The Pirate Bay has a whole host of movies available for people to download, oftentimes infringing on copyrights.

Even though you are producing a low-budget film, it doesn't mean that there won't be a lot of interest in the film ahead of the release. If there is, that DVD screener you produced for the distributors is like gold.

In the movie pirating business, new releases are generally put out on the Internet after they have been recorded by someone in the theater—usually in a foreign nation—using a video camera. The problem with these copies, , is that they are very low quality.

A DVD screener provides an excellent format for pirating. There have been plenty of films that have been available via pirate channels before their theatrical releases. Some of those were copied from DVD screeners. Unfortunately, we don't live in the world of *Mission: Impossible*, where the DVD screener could be set up to self destruct after viewing. It's going to be out there.

It's important that access to DVD screeners is tightly controlled. While a distributor is always going to cut into your profit margins a bit, having your film released as a pirated DVD screener before you even get a chance to sell tickets to see it is most certainly going to cut into your profits. Realize that this isn't the type of piracy where somebody will watch a bad cam copy of your film and be motivated to go see the film in a theater with the full experience of good sound and good video.

There have been some Hollywood executives who have suggested eliminating post-production screeners altogether. For the moment, these DVD screeners are the best way to get your movie in front of distributors and, because of that, you will be have to accept the risks. Be aware that controlling the channels through which those DVD screeners are distributed and knowing how many of them have been produced is imperative. Even for a small, low-budget film, there will

Distribution ■ *125*

be people out there who will be very interested in pirating your materials and distributing them over the Internet.

Refining the Package

Now that you know the basics of what you have, it's important to take a look at the types of things that are going to catch the eye of distributors. Because low-budget films are being discussed, it's not likely that the producer will be able to say that Brad Pitt or Jennifer Lawrence stars in the film, a factor that would immediately interest the distributor.

To start with, we'll address the poster.

The Poster

The poster for the film should suit the genre and communicate what the film is about. There are plenty of clichés in movie posters. Go through a DVD store and look at how many posters and DVD covers feature cleavage and guns.

If that suits the genre of your film, then it's probably a good idea to go with that sort of a poster. It will let the distributors know exactly what they will be promoting. If they know what they're promoting, they will know how to promote it effectively. For other types of films, a dramatic poster can make all the difference in people taking interest in the film.

A poster for a horror film should be chilling in some way. A poster for a drama should invoke emotions. A poster for a comedy should highlight the comedic premise. If it's raunchy, the poster should be a little bit raunchy. If it's a romantic comedy, it should be aimed at women or couples.

Brochures, etc.

If you're going to promote your film to distributors, utilize some of the same research that distributors will do themselves.

For example, in the previous chapter we talked about having movies pre-screened to get an idea of how audiences feel about them. One of the pieces of information you can include in your promotional materials is the information that you glean from those pre-screenings. For example, "Pre-screening audiences found that John Q Actor gave a performance that was memorable and engaging."

If you have materials related to testing out the general appeal of the film that were utilized before the film was produced, those might also be useful to include with a promotional package. Essentially, the distributor will want to know anything that will let them know about the film's commercially viability. If you have such materials, condense them into a form that is easily digestible. Make sure that it provides a good overview of the film and who it will appeal to.

Remember, while many film producers and other people involved in the art side of the filmmaking business have a generally dismal view of distributors, those distributors are in the business of making money. If anything you include as promotional material shows those distributors how they can make money off your film, it is more likely to capture their interest.

They will appreciate the arty aspects of the film , but they will also appreciate information that lets them know why they should put this film in their network of theaters. If you can tell them who will to be paying for the tickets, they have even more reason to believe that your film could be successful and want to stand behind it with their distribution network.

DVD Screener
A DVD screener is not a rough cut of the film. It should be, aside from any last-minute changes that are made due to focus group input, the final version of the film. The difference between it and the final version of the film is that the DVD screener will have a line across the bottom that lets audiences know that it is intended for screening purposes only. For example, you may see a line such as the following at the bottom of the DVD screener:

"For Screening Purposes Only. Not for Distribution."

The DVD screener should be packaged in a standard jewel case. This jewel case provides yet another opportunity to put compelling artwork on the product, potentially increasing the interest that the distributors will have in the movie. Because they may never unroll the film poster or go through any other materials you send, the cover on the DVD is vital.

If you're working with a consultant, they can have a graphic designer assemble a good cover for the DVD. Once you have the cover laid out, it's not particularly expensive to produce DVDs. You get a discount for producing them in quantity.

Remember that if you produce more DVDs of your screener, you have more screeners to control. There are also more screeners to be leaked. Ideally, have enough screeners to send to the distributors that you want to see the film and make absolutely certain you know who got those screeners and when.

To put this in the bluntest terms, if you happen to see your DVD screener show up on a pirate site, you're going to want to have a good idea how it got there so that you can go after the person who did it.

As an example of this, in 2009, a screener copy of the film *X-Men Origins: Wolverine* was leaked on the Internet. Some Internet sites were very responsible about this and they refused to deal with anyone who had watched one of the leaked copies and made a review of it. Fox News had one reviewer on staff who decided to go ahead and review the leaked copy.

First and foremost, the copy of *X-Men Origins* that leaked wasn't finished. This means that a review went out there based on a film that wasn't even completed. Friedman was fired by his employer for doing this, but the damage was done, nonetheless.

A Backdoor In

Let's, for a moment, imagine that your film is in a sort of worst-case scenario situation. It's a low-budget film, so it won't have the type of effects that an audience will expect in a blockbuster. It's a story-driven film, but there aren't any big-name actors in the movie, so you don't have the sort of prestige that comes with having a popular actor in your film.

There still may be a way for you to get your film into theaters, a lot of them, and to do so despite these challenges.

Anybody working in film production quickly finds out that a lot of the film industry is based on personal networks, personal favors, and politics in general. If you happen to have a low-budget film that was produced by a studio that has many high-budget, very desirable films to sell, you may be able to get your film in theaters by tying the distribution of your film to the distribution rights for a much more profitable film.

Obviously, this isn't something that you're likely to be able to set up yourself, given that you're the producer of a low-budget film and not the producer of a Hollywood blockbuster. Nonetheless, if you have the personal networks that make it seem like this could happen for you, it is definitely a route that you want to explore.

The film business is, in many ways, a business that could be described as less than ethical. There are a lot of favors that go on and, in exchange for those favors, the people that offer them generally expect that those favors will be paid back. If somebody owes you a favor, ask if they can give your movie something of a push among distributors and, if possible, if they could tie it to the distribution rights for a larger film. It's a long shot, but if it pays off, you could end up getting your film seen in many more theaters, and that could mean a lot more money.

Understanding What the Distributor Wants, and the Theaters

At this point, you have some idea of how to get your film viewed by distributors and what they're going to be looking for. What they're going to be looking for is profitability, .

You will be benefit from a greater understanding of what they are searching for. They are looking for a film that can pull in enough money to get them a worthwhile cut of the profits. It's a bit easier to understand film distribution if you understand where the money is going, as is the case with many things in life.

In the next section, we will go over the expenses that distributors and theaters incur when they pick up a film. What's important to understand is how they plan to profit from these films.

When you connect with a distributor, they will distribute that film to theaters. Every time that theater shows the film, they get a cut of the profits. One notch up the food chain, the distributor gets a cut from the theater. What's left over is what goes to the producer.

There may be other intermediaries involved. Whenever money moves between hands, there are plenty of people lining up to put themselves in the path of it. The more people involved in that path, the less money is left over for the producer.

Looking at the expenses that a distributor incurs will help you to understand how they view this entire transaction.

Prints

If a distributor decides to pick up your film, they will have to produce the prints that they will distribute to theaters. Each of these prints can cost thousands of dollars.

When you think about film distributors, thousands of dollars may not seem like a lot of money. However, with a big distribution deal, you might be looking at thousands of prints.

Many theaters today are chain operations. That means that the distributors may be selling the film to one individual who potentially represents thousands of different movie screens. These distribution deals can balloon in size very quickly and that means that the expenses for the distributor go up.

The distributor will also have to talk to the theaters buying the film to determine how much those theaters are willing to pay for it. This cuts out a portion of the distributor's profits, and they're going to want to make up for that somewhere. Likely, it's going to be by negotiating a larger cut for themselves as they kick money up to you.

Depending upon what type of film you have produced, the distribution deal may vary significantly in terms of how it is going to be set up. There are different strategies that are utilized to maximize the profits of the film.

Where figures are concerned, these are things that can be negotiated. For example, your distributor will charge you advertising costs on top of the percentage that they take from your film. One way you can keep this under control is to negotiate the advertising costs that they are allowed to bill you.

There is, unfortunately, another disadvantage built into this system for producers who make lower-budget films. If you have a film with a low budget, it's likely that the distributor will want a larger percentage of the profits. According to some sources, this can account for as much as 20% to 25% of the sales take for your films.

If you are not prepared to deal with the distributor yourself, you will be definitely want assistance with it. The contracts are complicated and there are many ways that you can end up having most of your profits taken away from you and handed to the distributor. There are many different costs that distributors can add to your contract, leaving you with very little.

In short, count on being charged for the following:

- *Marketing and promotion;*
- *Prints;*
- *"Administrative fees"—these are always vague;*
- *Translations, if needed.*

There are many ways that a distributor can bill you for services and you can be sure that they'll find a way to do it. Minimize tthese opportunities in your contract with them.

Time of Year Matters
If you're pitching a movie that has a very strong Christmas theme, you can be absolutely certain that the distributors are not going to want to start selling it to theaters so that they can show it in July. The time of year will make a difference in terms of when your film gets on theater screens.

Even people who aren't involved in the film industry generally know more about this than they are aware of. For example, everybody knows that summertime is when the movie theaters put out their huge blockbusters. If you have a low-budget film and you're competing with big-name stars in huge movies, any distributor worth their salt will understand that putting your movie on one of the multiplex screens is essentially a waste of that screen. They could easily put one of the summer blockbusters on that same screen, pack the theater for every single showing and sell a lot of popcorn, to boot.

Flash in the Pan or Enduring Story
A distributor will want to know how long your film will to remain popular in the theater. There is an easy formula for this that a lot of them go with.

If they were dealing with a big-budget release with big-name stars, it would be safe to assume that, on opening weekend, they would pull in a lot of money in ticket sales. This would happen regardless of whether or not the film held up over time. A film that holds up over time is said to have "legs." Essentially, it means that the film will consistently pull in good sales figures for the distributor and the theaters showing the film over the long haul.

A low-budget film is capable of having a big opening weekend and of having legs. Part of this will come down to how much promotion is given to the film before it is released into the theaters.

Promotion

Remember the advertising costs? If the distributor and the theaters don't promote your movie enough, it's not very likely that you're going to end up turning a profit on it. For example, if your movie was released in the summer and your film's poster was displayed next to much bigger posters, standees, and other promotional materials for the latest Marvel Comics film, you're probably not going to get the attention of much of the audience.

Scoring a distribution deal is a big accomplishment, but it doesn't necessarily mean that you are on the fast track to success. That movie still needs to be promoted and audiences still need to know that it is available for them to watch in theaters. They also need to know why they should go see this movie and why it has something to offer that the other movies do not.

Remember that distribution companies are worried about making money for themselves. If they can manage to recoup their costs and make enough of a profit for themselves, they're not particularly worried about whether or not you make a decent profit off of the movie that you put your hard work into.

Alternate Methods

As was previously mentioned, there are many filmmakers out there—particularly in the low-budget end of the film world—who are looking to find ways to distribute movies on their own. Some of them have found success doing this.

Distribution ■ *133*

The reason that they are interested in going this route quite simply is because distribution model used by Hollywood is broken. Not only is it broken, it is unnecessarily unfavorable to low-budget films. Films that have huge budgets get huge promotional efforts and, therefore, they predictably rake in huge profits. Low-budget films are generally relegated to showing later at night on smaller screens and, it's almost unheard of for them to be shown on more than one screen at a theater.

As we delve deeper into understanding distribution, keep in mind that there are definitely things about this system that make it much more amicable to larger movies. You will be be fighting an uphill battle, but there are some ways that you can maximize the chances that you will be get a good distribution deal that will prove to be profitable and worthwhile for you.

How Long Should a Distribution Deal Last?

A film distribution deal will come with a set amount of time that the distributors are allowed to sell your film to theaters. If there are ancillary rights included, it will also include a period of time during which they are allowed to distribute your movie on DVD and in other formats.

If you are a low-budget filmmaker, it's likely that the people in charge of distributing your movie aren't going to take your input all that seriously at times. They will decide how to best maximize the value of your movie with their distribution network.

One of the ways you can get around this is to use one of the distribution deals that involve using a consultant. This allows you to work with the distributor who doesn't treat you as if you are working for them; the opposite is true. If you become unhappy with the relationship with the distributor, you can simply end it whenever you want, provided that your contract is written in such a way.

The length of the distribution deal is something that you have to negotiate and the length must be based on your instincts. One requirement you can put into the contract is that you are entitled to a minimum amount of profit. In the event that the distributor is unable to provide that net amount to you, you would have the option to cancel the distribution deal and shop the film around to somebody else.

The thing to keep in mind: If you ink a bad distribution deal, you could be stuck with a substandard distributor for a very long time. If they put minimal effort into promoting your film—which may happen, if they don't believe that your film is capable of turning a decent profit for them—you may find yourself with a film that essentially rests in some sort of a limbo state, where it has distribution but no support and where it dies on the vine.

Crowd Sourcing Funds for Distribution
If you're hesitant to sign over the rights of your films to a distributor, or have been unsuccessful finding one, consider using a new resource, crowd-source funding.

One of the advantages with using this method is that you are relying on people who are likely to be fans of your film to help distribute it by providing funding. This can help create what is called, in Hollywood parlance, "buzz." This simply means that people are talking about the film, and that there is a lot of interest in the film, even before it has been released.

If you do plan to do your own distribution, the biggest barrier you're going to face is money. Even though the distribution model may be outdated and unfavorable to low-budget films, it is still the most effective way to get films on a theater screen. Whether it is the most effective way to make certain that the people who made a film turn a profit on it is arguable.

Domestic and Foreign
In order to distribute a film, you'll have to look into domestic and international distribution. For a clear illustration of why this is the case, one need look no further than the 2012 film *John Carter*.

This film was widely regarded as a complete flop in the United States. Looking at its box office gross there is something glaring that presents itself to the viewer about domestic and international distribution.

John Carter may have flopped domestically, but foreign gross for the film accounted for $211,061,000. Percentage wise, that means that *John Carter* took in a full 74% of its total gross from foreign sources. Foreign distribution is very important to the overall success or failure of a film, in the sense of how much money that the film makes.

Foreign distribution can be a boon to films that may not do well in the U.S.A. box office. To ink a foreign distribution contract, you'll need to work with a company that can get it seen in several different nations, and that will handle all the logistics of doing so. Like a domestic distributor, this distributor will take a cut of the profits, but will also supply you with agreed-upon forms of support for your film, such as foreign-language advertising.

Two film markets that reach foreign distributors are Cannes and MIPCOM. Cannes is held on the French Rivera and is, in addition to being one of the most important wheeling and dealing locations for Hollywood, the site of one of the most well-known film festivals in the world. It is a glamorous affair and it will cost you to get there, but it can be well worth it.

The festival takes place over the course of a little over a week. The buying and selling events are separate from the film festival. about everyone who's anyone will be here and, if you're the type of producer who loves to schmooze, this will be heaven.

MIPCOM is held in October. It is also held in Cannes, but it focuses on television distribution. If you're trying to get your film distributed to foreign television networks, this is the place to be, but it's not quite as glamorous as the Cannes Film Festival. Then again, few things are that glamorous.

Things to Keep in Mind About Foreign Distribution

Foreign distribution is complex. Primarily, if your film was shot in the US, it's most likely in English, possibly Spanish. This means that a translation of the film will have to be made for foreign audiences. This could be subtitles or dubbing, but this is a decision that you'll have to make.

You also need to keep in mind that some genres do not travel across cultural boundaries well. Action films tend to do very well. Everyone understands the concept of an action hero and, if you watch Bollywood films, Asian films, and so forth, you'll see how much action films from one part of the world influence action films from another. This genre tends to be easy to understand, no matter what one's cultural background might be.

Horror films also tend to do very well. Horror stories are universal and a scary villain's impact is not that much diminished by being from a different nation than the viewer. Michael Myers from *Halloween,* for example, is scary in any language. And one doesn't need to understand the dialogue to get the gist of the *Saw* movies.

Then, there are genres that don't travel well. Consider the romantic comedy. These films are staples of American summer theater screens and they tend to play on the same tropes over-and-over again. People expect to see those tropes, and they're willing to pay to see it.

Take one of those romantic comedies and export it overseas, and you may have a situation the audience won't get. Their culture may address romantic relationships much differently and the jokes that everyone in the US understands may be lost on a foreign audience.

Even when one considers how differently love and family are addressed in different cultural communities in the US, this is easy to see.

Films that are jingoistic, that deal with issues that are controversial in some nations—even if they're not in the US—and other culturally specific elements may make a film unsuitable for foreign distribution.

Foreign distributors will be looking for films that can turn them a profit and that means that they're going to be looking for films that will have a broad fan base in the nations where they distribute. A film that contains a lot of sex jokes will not go over well in nations where the culture tends to be very conservative about those things. You'll have to consider this when you're seeking out distribution.

Too Much Talking
One of the things you may have noticed about films that do well overseas, such as the aforementioned *John Carter*, is that those films aren't dialogue-heavy. Even if they do have a lot of dialogue, the subjects are simple and accessible.

John Carter is a guy who's trapped on Mars. He has a sword. There are bad guys. He has to kill the bad guys with the sword to save the pretty girl.

This isn't exactly Faulkner.
Where low-budget films are concerned, some of the best of the best are ones that rely on acting and a great script. If that great script is very dialogue-heavy and the concepts are very complex, they may not translate very well. Sometimes, truly great films belong to one language group because, when they're translated, they become oversimplified and lose much of their power.

The distributor will usually take care of the translation for you. It will be done in their nation with talented actors and native speakers, so everything will get done correctly, but correct doesn't always mean aesthetically true to the original vision.

If a foreign distributor thinks that your film won't work in their market because of language or cultural barriers, they may well be right. A film that does very well in Asia, for, instance, won't necessarily fill the seats in the Middle East.

The Logistics of Foreign Distribution

Your foreign distributor will be an entirely other entity from your domestic distributor. They will have their own contract terms and you will be have a specific set of obligations to them.

There are several ways you can approach this. One way is to pay for whatever distribution the company handles outright. This will mean that you get a flat payment for the rights to distribute the film and that, no matter how much the film makes, it goes to the distributor. On the good side of things, this means that there isn't much risk involved. If you sell the rights for $100,000 and the film only pulls in $50,000, you don't lose anything. Then again, if the film pulls in $300,000, you don't get any of the profit from the higher sales.

Another thing to keep in mind is that you're working at a disadvantage. Here's a quick example to make this apparent. You ink a deal to get a great low-budget action film distributed in Thailand. You know it will make money—it's about Thai boxing—and you know that, because you got part of the profits in your deal, that the money will start rolling in.

Can you read Thai? Because that's the language that you're likely to see the receipts in. You're also likely to be dealing with a currency exchange issue, so a very large weekend at the box office for your film may not amount to as much as you think.

Because of this complexity, many filmmakers prefer to sell the rights to their film outright and to let the foreign distributor handle the receipts and the rest of it. If the film bombs, the filmmaker still gets a tidy payment. If the film succeeds, that success can be used to market the film further in the domestic market or in other foreign markets and, , having a successful film gives one more leverage in negotiating future distribution contracts, including the lucrative rights to distribute the film on DVD and television.

Your Budget

Remember that the budget on which your film was made will make a difference in how much you get for the distribution rates. If your film was around the $5,000,000 ceiling that we're dealing with in this book, you stand to get a much higher payment than if it was a $400,000 film.

Lower-budget films, in short, mean that you'll have a distributor who wants a larger cut of the action, plus you'll likely have a harder time getting the film distributed widely. You can muster your resources, both business and personal, to make sure that you get a good deal and to make sure that your film has the best chances of succeeding, simply because it will get good distribution.

Straight to DVD

Having your film distributed straight to DVD is one of your options. According to *Variety*, the best-performing straight-to-DVD releases have been films that are sequels to larger films that had theatrical releases. These movies are released directly to DVD on the heels of a successful theatrical release. For films that don't have a prequel to rely on for recognition and that are low-budget to begin with, going straight to DVD could be a difficult route to profitability.

Declining Sales

They have been in decline in recent years. In addition to the much-publicized online piracy of copyrighted content, the demand for

DVDs overall has been declining. There are other options on the market now, and many viewers will prefer to watch films on Netflix, Hulu, or Amazon Prime, and any of the other streaming sites that allow them to get films instantly—no drive to the rental store—and not have to deal with storing and caring for a physical copy of the film in the future.

If you choose to go the DVD route, there are some things that you'll have to watch for. Those things can eat into your profits, oftentimes because, while a distribution deal of this type may have seemed great at the beginning, it will become apparent that, as always, there are people looking for ways to chew into your profits at the same time that they're claiming to offer you a service.

There is a self-distribution option where DVDs are concerned. You'll have to take care of details such as buying a UPC code for the film, and so forth, but this option is more suitable for micro-budget or indie fare that has little chance of ever getting an audience outside of a very specific demographic. Where a film in the $400,000 to $5,000,000 range is concerned, there are better options.

It's also important to keep in mind that direct-to-DVD fare doesn't have the favor among critics, who will be important for providing publicity for your film, particularly if you get good reviews. Direct-to-DVD movies have something of a B-movie reputation and, in addition to the fact that demand for DVDs is declining, anyway, that may make it particularly difficult to work profitably with this distribution model.

What to Watch For

A theatrical distributor may well want you to give them the rights to distribute your film on DVD, as well as in theaters. If you have this option, it will be covered under the Grant of Rights section in your contract.

If you used a foreign distributor to get in on the lucrative overseas market, it's likely that you already have given them the rights to

Distribution ▪ *141*

distribute your film on DVD as part of your contract. This can be a very good thing, as it allows you to avoid having to work with the logistics of distribution in foreign markets.

Domestically, you may find yourself in a situation where getting theatrical distribution for your film is very difficult, due to the reasons noted in the previous section. In such cases, going direct-to-DVD is an option, but keep the following in mind, which are also addressed in more detail below:

- *How much of a cut of the profits you get;*
- *How long the distribution contract lasts for;*
- *How much marketing the company will do for your film.*

To get a broad overview of the importance of these questions, one need only envision the following scenario. Your film ends up languishing on DVD store shelves and online sites with no promotion. The company not promoting it owns the rights to it for the next 20 years. When it does sell a copy, you get a pittance, if anything. You do not want to end up in that situation.

Look Into the Company
There are any number of companies out there who will offer to distribute your film on DVD. Not all of them are the sort of companies that you'd want to do business with.

Look into their reputation online. You can do this very easily by Google searching the company and seeing what comes up. In the case of bad companies that do not promote the films that they distribute and that do not pay the filmmakers a suitable amount for ownership of the film, you'll usually start to see pages come up that were written by angry filmmakers.

Keep in mind that these filmmakers themselves may be incompetent. They may have inked a deal without understanding it, or made any of a number of other mistakes that plague beginning filmmakers. With a budget starting at several hundred thousand dollars you have no excuse to make such a mistake. Do your research. If you're not sure what a contract says, get a lawyer to look at it. It's usually not particularly expensive to get a lawyer to spend an hour or two going over a contract so they can figure out whether or not you're getting a good deal.

Expenses

Like a theatrical distributor, a direct-to-DVD distributor will bill you for every expense that they rack up promoting your film, if you let them get away with it. There are oftentimes vagaries in the contracts such as "administrative fees." Be wary of these.

Again, make sure you negotiate a maximum amount that the distributor can charge you in marketing fees. This helps to ensure two things. One, you don't end up getting charged for extravagant, ineffective marketing schemes. Two, you don't end up having to pay so much to the company that you cannot possibly make a profit off of the film.

Watch the Books

Have some access to the books that the distributor keeps on your film. You should receive financial information at regular intervals: quarterly, twice per year, every year, whatever works for you. The idea here is that you can see a breakdown of the expenses and profits from the film so that, if something isn't right, you can catch it with your own accountants.

Your distributor should, at the very least, be willing to give you regular reports on the sales and expenses, if they don't let you see their books directly.

Packaging Control

Make sure you have at least some control over how the film is packaged. A direct-to-DVD distributor, if they're releasing your film as one of a number that they're distributing at the same time, may go with generic artwork and unattractive packaging, which can cost you sales.

Distribution ■ *143*

Ideally, the DVD release will be packaged so that it fits perfectly with the rest of your marketing efforts. This ensures that you get good branding for the film, from the original artwork on the poster to the font that's used on the DVD package.

How You're Paid
Some direct-to-DVD distributors will go with an advance model for payment and some will give you a cut of the profits from the film.

If you're being paid an advance, the entire process is very easy. You get your check, they get their rights and that's the end of it. If you're getting paid on the gross receipts, the situation is remarkably different.

This is where paying attention to the expenses is particularly important. You'll need to be certain that you know what expense has to be paid back to the company before you start seeing payments from the profits on the film.

You also need to know when you're going to get paid. This will be worked out in the contract. If you don't hammer this out adequately beforehand, you might find yourself waiting too long for checks from the sales of your film and putting up with other hardships that could make a potentially profitable relationship into an utter disaster.

Indie Distribution
If your film is in the Art House category, you may end up going the independent distribution route. There are out there that can help you with this, but some of the same concerns apply as would if you were working with a direct-to-DVD distributor.

Make sure you know what you're being charged for and how much. Also make certain that you know about every single cut that's coming out of your profits, who it's going tom and why they're getting it.

For low-budget films, indie distribution should not be a concern. Even though $400,000 to $5,000,000 films are low-budget by

Hollywood standards, even the low end of that figure, if someone were to earn it over the course of a year, is easily in excess of an upper-class income. This is a lot of money and, even though it might not be the type of money that could fund the next *Thor* movie, it's still enough to insist on having the support to get legitimate distribution.

How You End Up Going Direct-to-DVD

For a film producer, hearing that their film is going direct-to-DVD is oftentimes like hearing a doctor say that they've been diagnosed with a fatal illness. It can sometimes sound like the film has not turned out that well and there is some truth to this. There are many different reasons that a film may end up going direct-to-DVD, but not all of them mean that it's over for the film. That direct-to-DVD decision on the part of a studio may be changed, in some cases.

Low Predicted Performance

In upcoming sections, we'll deal with film festivals. Some low-budget films debut at film festivals and become crowd favorites, practically securing their theatrical distribution right there. This isn't always how it turns out, however.

In some cases, after a test screening or a showing at a film festival, the studio behind a film, or even the producer themselves may decide that the film doesn't have much of a chance in the theatrical market. In such cases, they may take the film directly to a DVD release to skip the expenses of a theatrical release. This is a very hard decision to make, as it means that the film's overall promotional efforts essentially end right there. All the buzz about the film ends up with it being on DVD store shelves, anyway, and no producer likes to see that happen. Neither do the investors in the films.

Controversial Content

In the section on movie ratings, the way the MPAA works and the impact that ratings have on movies in terms of their theatrical distribution was discussed. Sometimes, a direct-to-DVD film ends up that way because the artistic vision is determined to be more important than getting the film distributed in theaters.

Controversial content can be included on a DVD without the hassles that might come with putting that content on a theater screen. The theater chain, in essence, doesn't have to risk its reputation by playing content that could result in a lot of problems, lost profits, and so forth.

In some cases, compromising the artistic vision of the film to satisfy theatrical distributors may be deemed not worth it by the producer and others involved in the making of the film. In such cases, going direct-to-DVD may enable the film to be released—with a significant diminishing in potential profits—with controversial scenes intact.

This is down to whether or not any needed compromises required to get a rating are deemed worth it by the producer and other people behind the film. It's possible to go unrated on a DVD release and to still include whatever original content was written into the script.

Very Niche

Some films in the low-budget range are so niche that there's no way that a distributor will look at them as viable theater candidates. These aren't necessarily micro-budget films, either, and they sometimes have substantial amounts of money behind them. Going direct-to-DVD has proven to be a successful model for some studios.

Tromaville is an example of this. This studio produces a great deal of direct-to-DVD fare and has gotten a cult following with releases such as *The Toxic Avenger*, *Sgt. Kabukiman N.Y.P.D.*, and *Mother's Day*. These films are not blockbusters nor are they the types of films that will appeal to the general moviegoer. They are true to their visions, that being of raunchy, gory, violent exploitation flicks.

If your film ish one that will have a niche audience and little appeal outside of that audience, going direct-to-DVD might be a very good option, though it means not getting in on potentially lucrative theater distribution.

A Sequel

As was mentioned, big studios sometimes produce low-budget sequels to movies that have done very well at the box office. These are oftentimes released direct-to-DVD. They oftentimes also have much lower production appeal and quality than their predecessors and rely on the audience's familiarity with and desire to see more of an established character or universe.

In cases where your low-budget film is one of these types, going direct-to-DVD might be the best option and the only one the funders are willing to stand behind. This isn't a bad thing, necessarily, as the film will still have the prestige of a known title behind it to boost the sales of the DVDs.

In these cases, the fact that the film is going direct-to-DVD will generally be established at the start and theatrical distribution will not become an issue at any point.

Direct to Digital

As was said, sales of DVDs have been in decline. As is the case with the music industry, the movie industry has been changing as physical media has fallen out of favor with consumers. Digital downloads and streaming viewing are both huge today and they can be important to distributing a film.

There are many companies that specialize in distributing films digitally. There are also several venues that are particularly important to this distribution method. They include:

- *Amazon;*
- *Hulu;*
- *Netflix.*

Distribution ■ *147*

These sites allow a mix of free films that are supported with advertising, subscription models that allow viewers to choose from a vast library of films and even rental programs—in the case of Amazon—that allow viewers to rent the film and watch it within a given period of time before the rental expires and the film is no longer available.

This has some significant advantages for getting a film seen. Principally, it makes the film more available. Streaming content can be viewed on:

- *Televisions;*
- *Tablet computers;*
- *PCs;*
- *Smartphones.*

This availability may result in more sales. The trick is that you have to keep your eye on the money, where it's going and why.

Where direct-to-digital is concerned, the things to watch out for are much the same as what you would have to watch out for if you were going direct-to-DVD. You will be want to make certain that you are getting a worthwhile cut of any sales or rentals of your film.

You'll also want to make sure that you're not paying too much for marketing the film. It's very easy for a company to put up a simple website to market your film for download, pay a few hundred dollars for it, and bill you thousands in fees.

Digital distribution is a very "right now." There is good reason for this. For some consumers, there are pros and cons that make one of these options far preferable to the other and, increasingly, they're going with digital.

Digital access to film doesn't require shipping, a trip to the store, or any other effort on the part of the consumer. It also doesn't require that the consumer choose from whatever the store happens to have available on their shelves. Sites such as Netflix have literally thousands of films available, and they span all genres.

Digital access also doesn't require that the consumer take care of a DVD. And it doesn't expose the consumer to a significant—and annoying—drawback of physical formats: outdated formats.

While some filmmakers may have reservations about digital distribution, remember that it does make a difference to the bottom line. It means that they don't have to rebuy the same content when the format preference moves from VHS to DVD to Blu-ray to whatever else is coming next. The format is independent of a dedicated player.

Packaging
Digital distribution involves the same packaging concerns that go along with theatrical and DVD distribution. There needs to be good cover art, which will be a thumbnail of the film's cover that is displayed on distribution sites, in most cases. The film's poster is a good choice for this.

There also needs to be excellent copy for the film so that people are enticed to download it, rent it, or stream it. This can be the same copy that is used for the rest of the marketing campaign, but be aware that, on streaming sites, the copy has to be particularly good. There are plenty of other films out there that the subscribers can watch and getting them to watch yours may be difficult if your copy is lacking.

Making a Deal
A flat-fee distribution deal for digital distribution can be very useful. It's another source of income from the film, and it can help to get the film seen.

Take a look at sites like Amazon and you'll see a huge library of movies. The same is true of Netflix, Hulu, and other streaming sites. These sites are in ferocious competition with one another and,

Distribution

because of that, they do offer some good options. If your digital distribution is handled by the same entity that handles another form of distribution for you, all of this is easier, but it's still important to be aware of how much money is being taken out of what would otherwise be the cut for the people who made the film.

References:

http://www.howstuffworks.com/movie-distribution.htm

http://www.nytimes.com/2010/01/17/movies/17dargis.html?_r=0

http://www.huffingtonpost.com/2013/01/09/oscar-screeners-most-pirated_n_2434507.html

http://www.hollywoodreporter.com/blogs/thr-esq/summit-anti-piracy-exec-dvd-58029

http://www.filmthreat.com/features/24146/

http://www.gcglaw.com/resources/entertainment/film_distribution_deals.html

http://variety.com/2012/digital/news/direct-to-dvd-films-decline-1118050065/

http://blogs.indiewire.com/shadowandact/direct-to-dvd-market-sales-in-decline

http://www.megalodon.com/cd-dvd-barcode-distribution.html

http://www.danosongs.com/blog/7-indie-film-digital-distribution-companies-you-can-submit-to-online/

http://news.cnet.com/8301-33620_3-57564914-278/keep-your-blu-rays-and-dvds-hollywood-ive-gone-digital/

Chapter 8

Film Festivals and Markets

Up until now, the film industry on the whole has been demonstrated to be full of business norms and practices that favor films with larger budgets and bigger studios behind them. There is one venue where low-budget films have an advantage. Film festival goers love low-budget movies.

Film markets are entirely commercial events, covered at the end of this chapter. Getting into these events is generally a matter of having the money required and getting in on time.

Festivals Overview

For many low-budget film producers, getting into a notable film festival is one of their primary goals. Winning an award at a prestigious film festival is even more desirable. Both of these things can have real value in terms of facilitating the distribution, and eventual success, of a film that may not have been particularly profitable otherwise.

If the process of distribution had seemed like an uphill battle before, there are good things to be found in how film festivals can fit into the distribution and profitability of a low-budget film. Film festival audiences are generally enthusiastic about the idea that truly great films can be made on modest budgets and that good storytelling can outweigh the value of visual spectacle and even big-name stars.

Quality, low-budget films can get a lot of publicity at film festivals and, on top of that, wheeling and dealing is completely acceptable at these events.

With all of that being said, getting into a film festival doesn't maximize your chances of getting a great distribution deal, meaningful publicity, or anything else.

Finding the Right Festivals

There's something of an irony about film festivals. While they tend to espouse and embody a very egalitarian view about the art of filmmaking, there is also a hierarchy with these festivals. Some festivals are international events where multi-million dollar deals are routinely made; others are utterly insignificant.

Types of Film Festivals

Film festivals come in different types. For a film between $400,000 and $5,000,000 total budget, it's likely that the film is either an independent film or a film that was produced by a large studio as a feature, but which was a lower-budget feature.

There are independent film festivals that are designed to showcase work produced outside of the large-studio, feature-film world. These festivals can help propel a film that may not have otherwise gotten a lot of attention to become very successful.

There are also film festivals for feature films produced by large studios. These are held in the US and in Europe and are typically the subjects of a lot of media coverage.

Below are some of the largest festivals of each type.

Notable Film Festivals

Cannes International Film Festival

Held: Early in the year, typically in May

Location: Cannes, France

Description: This is one of the largest and most prestigious of all film festivals worldwide. Some very well-known and successful films, including *Sex, Lies and Videotape* and *The Pianist* have won the top honor at this festival, the Palme d'Or. This festival is an invitation-only affair and it's not easy to get in. The film showings at this festival are attended by the biggest on- and off-screen players in Hollywood and in European cinema, so it's definitely a place to see and be seen, if you can get in. The good news is that films that are heady, story-driven and well-made, even if they are made on a smaller budget than the blockbuster films Hollywood puts out, can do very well here. This festival is a centerpiece in the world of European cinema.

Venice Film Festival

Held: August-September

Location: Lido, Venice, Italy

Description: This is generally regarded as one of the most important film festivals worldwide. The top award is the Golden Lion and some notable films from the US have taken it home, including *Brokeback Mountain*. This film festival is good for very serious films, arty films and films from any nation.

Berlin International Film Festival

Held: February

Location: Berlin, Germany

Description: This is a huge festival and is as prestigious as it is popular. Hundreds of thousands of visitors come to this festival every year, which means a lot of exposure for films that get featured here. It is particularly important for the European market and there are events held all over the city at the same time as the festival, where deals are made and rights sold. Good films from all over the world compete for awards here, and some of the winners include *The Thin Red Line*, *Rain Man* and many other well-known movies.

San Francisco International Film Festival

Held: Spring

Location: San Francisco, CA, USA

Description: This is the oldest film festival currently running in the US. It's a great venue for films that are looking for a distribution deal and tens of thousands of people come to the Bay Area during the festival. It offers several awards and recognitions and includes informational events about the film industry and how it's evolving.

Toronto International Film Festival

Held: September

Location: Toronto, Ontario, Canada

Description: This film festival is popularly known as TIFF. This is one of the world's leading film festivals and one of the best ones to be featured in. TIFF is basically the Cannes of North America. The People's Choice award that is given out every year has included some very successful films. This is not a competition festival, so there's no golden this or that to win, but the festival is one that can launch a film to much greater success.

Seattle International Film Festival

Held: May-June

Location: Seattle, WA, USA

Description: This festival draws over 100,000 people and is one of the best-known festivals on the North American continent. It has a very different feel and even features a Secret Festival event, where seeing films means that you cannot talk about them, and that you'll have no idea what you're going to watch until you've seen it. This is a competitive festival with a jury and several awards are given out. The best films get the Golden Space Needle.

Sundance Film Festival

Held: January

Location: Utah, USA

Description: Getting into this film festival is a goal for many indie filmmakers. This film festivalis specifically intended for independent films and it's one of the most prestigious film festivals of that type in North America. Some of the best-known directors currently working in Hollywood got their first real chance at success here, and it's an important place for making connections.

SXSW (South by Southwest)

Held: Spring

Location: Austin, TX, USA

Description: A film festival is one part of what goes on at SXSW. It's also a tech conference, a business networking opportunity, an educational event and more. The word that describes it best is probably "hip." The film festival is geared toward new names in the industry. Low-budget films that feature a good, unknown director may stand a real chance of getting some recognition at this particular festival.

Tribeca Film Festival

Held: Spring

Location: Lower Manhattan, New York City, NY, USA

Description: This is a relatively new festival but it already draws approximately 3 million people to its doors. The festival has more than 1,000 screenings and features films from across a wide variety of genres. The festival is set up to get independent films exposed to a wider audience, so it's an obvious choice for low-budget films that were made outside of the major studios.

Getting Into a Festival;

Anyone in the role of producer has some business sense, in all likelihood. Even though film festivals are, in many regards, about the art of filmmaking, pretending that these aren't very much business-friendly venues is naive. The first part of selling a film is knowing your audience and, likewise, the first part of getting into a festival is knowing the festival audience.

Pick the Festival

If you have a great indie film that you're trying to get distributed, you're not going to have much luck getting into the major film festivals, such as Cannes, without a lot of connections to make that happen.

The best way to approach a festival where you don't have any real connection to someone who can get you in is to take a look at what the festival is about. Make sure you can honestly say that the film festival is made to showcase films such as your own.

If you're promoting an indie production, Sundance, Tribeca, and other independent film festivals will be your best bets. The audience will likely be favorable to them if it's good. If you've got a production with some clout behind it, even if the budget is low, you may be able to get into TIFF or another major festival.

Submissions

There may very well be a fee for submitting your film to the festival. If you cannot afford the fee, you might be able to get someone to sponsor the entry for you.

The submissions will be subject to strict guidelines. You'll have to make sure that your film adheres to these guidelines in every regard. This may include the content of the film, the length of the film, the format and so forth.

There will be a deadline for submissions and this won't be negotiable. Make sure you get the film in well before the deadline and verify that everything required was received.

VERY IMPORTANT: Some film festivals require that your film have its world premiere at their festival. This means that you may disqualify yourself from one festival by participating in another. Make sure you check to see if this is a requirement. Obviously, if you have a choice between premiering at Sundance or a smaller, less significant festival, you'd want to pull your film from consideration at the smaller festival and premiere at Sundance.

Packaging
Packaging is a vital component of the movie promotion process to distributors and consumers, but it's not at film festivals. You don't have to spend money on a package to promote your film. There's a good chance that your additional materials won't even be seen by the people screening the film, so you can concentrate on getting them the film in the format that they require.

Don't Be a Movie Star
While having connections might help you at some festivals, it won't at others. You're not going to automatically be chosen for the schedule over three other films simply because they all had lower budgets than you. When you're dealing with people, trying to name-drop and use other methods of getting "in" probably won't help much at these venues.

Be Prepared to Wait
Some film festivals get literally tens of thousands of submissions every year. The staff has to screen all of these and determine from among them which to include in the festival. This takes time, but you'll find out by the deadline.

There may be a situation where you'll have to make the decision referenced above regarding premieres, but in a more high-pressure scenario. If you have a chance of getting into Sundance, but you don't know, and a smaller but still good, film festival wants you to premiere at their event, it could be tough.

This comes down to risk and reward and, as is the case with all such wagers, it comes down to what the decision-making parties want to do and what they feel they have to gain or lose from any outcome.

Premiering at a Festival
Anyone who has been in the film business for longer than five minutes probably knows that premieres are huge events. For major motion pictures, they oftentimes involve red carpets, gaggles of press and a lot of celebrity guests.

Due to requirements or simply because you planned it that way, you may be having your premiere at the festival itself. This is a chance to promote the film; don't miss out on it.

What the Premiere Means
There's a lot of debate as to whether or not it's a good thing that film festivals require many participants to have their film premiere at the festival. What is generally accepted is that the reason that festivals have this requirement is simple: publicity. The premiers are great ways to get industry players to the festival and, for anyone promoting a film, that's advantageous.

Film festivals, particularly the best-known ones, are important networking events for film industry people. Having a film premiere at one of these festivals, and having it go over particularly well is a great way to generate buzz for a film.

If you're getting a red-carpet premiere at the festival, play it up as much as you can. Make sure you're ready to network. If someone is impressed with your film and they have some clout, feel free—obligated, if you want to make the most of it—to buy them a drink, dinner, or engage in whatever other schmoozing you can to keep them interested in your film.

What to Do After You Premiere

Obviously, a lot of film festivals will be off-limits to you after you do premiere at one of them. This doesn't mean that give up on the film festival circuit. There are plenty of film festivals every year and there are new ones that pop up all the time.

If you can get into the better ones, you'll still find that you can get the film exposed to new, and important, audiences.

Understanding the Vibe

If you want to wheel and deal, the film markets are the places to be. If you want to participate in a festival, meet people and have fun, see films other than your own and, perhaps, get a huge boost for your film, the film festivals are the places to be.

When you're at the film festival, remember that it's not the film market. When you schmooze, not everything should be about business. These are art events and they're great places to get your film closer to being a success, but they're not the kind of places where people like to feel like they're doing business all the time. They might be doing business all the time, but they don't want to *feel* that way.

If your film captures someone's interest and they want to talk to you about picking up distro rights or other business, it's a great opportunity, but it's not the entire point of a film festival.

Film Market Overview

What if you do want to wheel and deal and don't want to concentrate on awards, premieres and the rest of it?

Consider the film markets. These are trade shows and huge ones at that. It's all about making deals, making money and getting great products out there for the viewing public. They're worth attending for anyone promoting a film who can afford to participate.

The American Film Market
This event is held in Santa Monica, CA. It's a huge event, with nearly 10,000 people showing up every year. The entire point of the event is to facilitate the film industry. There are people buying films at this event, people selling films and people who are looking to get new films produced.

The festival is held in November and is associated with the Independent Film and Television Alliance. This is one of the largest and most important film industry events of the year in North America.

Asian Film Market
This takes place in the autumn in Busan, South Korea and is one of the premier events for getting in on the Asian market. The events include showcases and screenings, along with exhibitors and a host of other happenings that provide great networking and selling opportunities.

MIPCOM
This festival takes place in Cannes. The festival opens up doors to the television market, which is great for getting distribution for movies that may have already had or never will have a theatrical release. The festival is held in the autumn, usually in October.

The Cannes Film Market
If you don't have an invitation to the Cannes Film Festival, you can come to the Cannes Film Market. This marketplace is set up for business and everyone who works in the film industry in any high-level capacity, particularly in the European market, will to be here or to wish they could be. This is a great place to make deals for the European market and, because it takes place at the same time as the festival, the potential is only increased.

Participating in the Markets
Participating in these markets can cost thousands of dollars, easily. There are options for booth displays that can get a lot of interest but,

it's also a gamble, in that you may not get a deal to recoup the costs of participating.

There will generally be different areas where participants can set up booths, have movie screenings and so forth. These marketplaces sometimes take over several different properties at the same time, given the thousands of people who attend them.

Some of these festivals, such as the American Film Market, allow you to have if you purchase a booth. Each festival will have its own policies.

Each festival will also have a cutoff date for entries, so be sure you know it if you want to shop your film around at these festivals. If you have a booth, be sure you have posters, brochures and other information about the film that you're trying to market.

Film festivals and film markets are both great ways to promote a film, but are also very different things. For some producers, getting the word out about a film means investing in attending some of these events. Winning a festival can be a reward on its own, but it can also open plenty of new doors.

Remember that the connections you stand to make at these festivals can be vitally important to future projects, even if the current project fails to win recognition at the festival. Your world premiere may not be the packed event that you have hoped it would be, but that doesn't mean that your film will go unappreciated and, , it's easier to step through a door that you've already opened once, and you may have a chance to benefit from participating in a film festival in a way that isn't realized the first time you attend.

References:

http://www.filmindependent.org/blogs/want-to-get-your-film-into-sundance-the-festivals-programmers-reveal-secrets-to-successful-submissions/

Chapter 9

Additional Information

A great deal of information has been covered thus far. Unfortunately, where the film industry is concerned, the degree of complexity with any project is so high that something always gets left out. This applies to every element of the production process. From the moment the script is conceived to the point where the film has finished its theatrical run and heads off to the online streaming sites, there is always more to learn and more to do.

This chapter will fill in some areas where more information is needed. This information could apply to any part of the production process rather than to one particular phase. Contracts will come into play during the preproduction, production, and post-production phases, so there's no sense in putting that information in just one section.

The information contained in this section should help any producer understand how deals are secured and what owning rights means.

The film industry, even for the most experienced players, is always full of surprises. When it comes to making sure you get paid and retain ownership of the things that pay your wages, surprises are never good things.

When You Need a Lawyer

Sometimes producers will need to contract services from lawyers. This is inevitable, as there is so much money that changes hands when movies are made and that much money changing hands means that there is always room for a heated dispute.

Entertainment lawyers are specialist attorneys that work in this field. They work with producers, actors, studios, and everyone else involved, but specialize in claims and contracts that are specific to the entertainment industry. This makes them valuable assets to anyone in this business, particularly the person responsible for putting the entire movie together, who has to rely on contracts being honored, cuts being paid and so forth.

Film producers will want entertainment lawyers who specialize in film. There are lawyers in this industry who specialize in working with musicians, and their work may differ substantially from a film lawyer's work.

Demystifying the Entertainment Lawyer

Entertainment lawyers have good PR for themselves, which can make them seem like the ultimate narrators of everything in Hollywood, as well as the film industry everywhere else.

They're vital, but they're like everyone else in the film industry. As the electrician on a movie set is a skilled tradesperson who has a specialized and necessary understanding of the film industry, an entertainment lawyer is lawyer like any other—hopefully better than most—who has a very in-depth knowledge of the entertainment industry.

This allows entertainment lawyers to handle things that will be of particular concern to film producers. Before one starts thinking of

Additional Information

entertainment lawyers as celebrities in and of themselves, it's important to realize what they are. They're good lawyers who understand the film business.

You want one who meets both criteria to a higher standard than the average lawyer can claim, .

What They Do

The first and most important thing that a lawyer will do for you is to help you draft contracts. You're going to need contracts for:

- *Cast;*
- *Crew;*
- *Director;*
- *Distributors;*
- *DVD distributors;*
- *Buying rights;*
- *Selling rights;*
- *Merchandizing rights.*

This is all very specialized work. Successful entertainment lawyers can sometimes become very wealthy, simply because not everyone can do this type of work and it requires such a broad knowledge of a particular industry and very complex and in-depth understanding of the law that applies to that industry.

Here are some of the things that a lawyer can do for a producer.

Unions

Many films are union operations. Dealing with unions can be tough and there are very high standards expected by the people working on the film in regards to their working conditions and how they're paid. The unions protect the worker's interests and, sometimes, the producer will need a lawyer to protect their own.

The lawyer can handle problems with the unions, if they arise, and make sure the project stays on track.

Cast

Actors will want to negotiate their interest in the film and the lawyer can make sure that everything is written down in accordance with what has been agreed upon. This makes everything work more smoothly for everyone involved in the film and ensures that everyone's getting the deal that they agreed to.

Liability

Ask any stunt person: films can be dangerous. Lawyers ensure that your production has everything it needs in terms of liability protection and that all your bases are covered so that you can avoid being sued. They also do this by making sure agreements with financiers are fully understood and not written in a way that puts the production at a disadvantage.

Ownership

Intellectual property is a huge concern in the film industry. Entertainment lawyers understand how it works. They know when you have the right to go after someone for infringement and when you do not. There is much more extensive information on intellectual property later in the chapter, and this is one of the most significant reasons that it's important to have a good lawyer available to you.

Getting a Lawyer

Getting a lawyer is a bit like getting an agent. There are plenty of entertainment lawyers out there, as there are plenty of agents out there. A further similarity is that some of the options are very, very bad choices.

Some of the criteria for picking an entertainment lawyer will disqualify or qualify them immediately:

The Right Area of Practice

What you'll be looking for is a contract lawyer. If you have to sue someone, this lawyer will sometimes handle that, but that will hopefully not become a concern. A lawyer who understands entertainment industry contracts is what's needed on a day-to-day basis.

Time in the Industry
The entertainment industry is full of ways to get ripped off. A lawyer who has been at it as an entertainment lawyer for some time will likely notice when someone is trying to take you for a ride. You'll want someone who has been working in the entertainment industry for a long time.

Availability
Not every lawyer will be available to you. Some of them will have very high-paying clients and you will be not be able to afford what those lawyers charge. If they already have a full roster of clients, even if you could afford them, they may not have time to represent you.

For a low-budget film, a very expensive, high-powered lawyer will be out of the question, but there are ways that you can get a lot for your money and, by exploiting your personal networks, you may be able to get a great lawyer.

Talk to Friends
Personal networks are huge assets for producers. If one has a good network, asking contacts about good lawyers that work with low-budget films may be a good way to find someone. You may be able to get all of your contracts and other legal requirements hammered out competently for an affordable sum.

You might even be able to get a very high-priced lawyer to help you at a good rate for being a friend of a friend or for having another connection.

At the very least, ask around about any lawyer you're considering. If no one's ever heard of them, it's one thing, but if everyone has and it's not good, that information could save you a lot of problems in the future.

Education

Organizations offer specialized training for entertainment lawyers. It's not a bad idea to ask any lawyer you're unsure of if they've had this type of training.

If You Have to Sue

Threatening to sue someone is rather a staple of the film industry. It is not hard to find experienced litigators in the entertainment industry. The thing to keep in mind is that your contract lawyer will not likely handle this at all.

If you do have to sue or if you are sued, you'll want someone with experience litigating in entertainment industry disputes. Remember that this attorney may well be the person who determines—by their skill at litigating—whether or not you get your fair share of profits from your film, whether your intellectual ownership is honored, and other important issues. Get someone good, and make sure that the lawyers who handle drawing up your contracts are competent, ensuring that your litigation lawyer doesn't have to try to argue a bad case.

Intellectual Property

Intellectual property is one of the most important concepts in filmmaking. Films are works of art. Commercial art, in many cases; but films are works of art, nonetheless. This means that they fall under the category of intellectual property and that means that the laws that apply to intellectual property are of paramount importance to producers.

What It Is and Isn't

Copyright protection is what allows a business entity or an individual to take something artistic they created, legally declare and make known that it is theirs and to, therefore, get profits from it. This law is one of the foundational concepts that makes the film industry one of the most profitable industries in the world. Without copyright protection, anyone could take your work, reproduce, and sell it however they wished, and not give you a dime.

Additional Information ■ *169*

That part of about giving you a dime is why intellectual ownership is so relentlessly fought over in the industry. Whoever owns the intellectual property can profit from it and everyone wants a share if they feel that they own a piece of it.

It Can Get You Sued

Sometimes, people use the court system to assert their rights, get money to which they are entitled and stand up against people who would have otherwise ripped them off. In other cases, people sue frivolously, trying to get money or publicity. Either way, productions sometimes get sued due to copyright claims.

Generally, these types of lawsuits follow a similar pattern. A movie is about to be made or released and someone comes forward and claims that the script was stolen from one of their original ideas. In 2011, for example, a screenwriter Disney and Pixar, claiming that a film they were about to release had stolen ideas from a script of his to which the companies had access.

This isn't uncommon and it's another reason why it's so important to make sure that the script you're starting with is truly original. If it turns out someone sold you a script that was ripped-off from someone else, the original writer may come after the production with a lawsuit, and they may have a very good reason to do so.

If the person going after you happens to have a copyright that you didn't know about, the situation can be bad.

Understanding Infringement

Infringement of copyright is one of the hottest issues in the news right now. Generally, it's the entertainment industry—not beleaguered screenwriters or authors—that is suffering from it.

Copyright infringement occurs whenever someone has a copyrighted work distributed, sold, performed or otherwise made accessible to the public without their permission. For many Hollywood films, this means being distributed over the Internet without the studio—and, hence, the producers and others—getting paid for their work.

If productions or studios get sued, it's usually because someone claims that the studio took their work and made a movie out of it. This can end up costing a lot of money if the claim is valid. Remember that, simply because a film cost $5,000,000 at the most to make, that doesn't mean that it won't be profitable. See *The Blair Witch Project* for a clear illustration of this.

Getting Permission

If you're in doubt, get permission. If you're not sure whether or not a piece of work that you want to use—whether it's music, dialogue or something else—is copyrighted, ask your attorney to look into it.

It's best to avoid making any assumptions in this regard.

Once you do have your film completed, you have to make sure that the rights are secured. If you're working with a studio, the studio's lawyers will likely take care of this. You certainly won't have to file a copyright on your own.

It's still a good idea to understand how this process works, however. In the case of indie films, it is possible to end up not owning the work that you produced, though this is harder to do these days that it was not too long ago.

Own Your Film: Don't End Up Like *Night of the Living Dead*

This story that follows is particularly relevant to the topic of this book, given the budget that the film being discussed was shot on and the commercial and cultural importance that the film embodies.

Night of the Living Dead is a legendary film. It's a low-budget film shot in 1968. The original budget was $114,000, which is equivalent to $740,000 in 2012 dollars. That puts it at the lower end of the budgets that the films being addressed in this book would be expected to have.

Night of the Living Dead got hardly any money for writer and director George Romero. The film is responsible for launching the entire modern zombie genre, which anyone knows has turned out to be incredibly lucrative for the film industry. From the slow-walking, dazed cannibals of the 1960s and 1970s to the flesh-eating monsters in hit shows such as *The Walking Dead* and even video games such as *Killing Floor*, Romero is owed a debt. The movie that spawned it all was the victim of a minor copyright flub.

In 1968, the law still required that, to have a valid copyright on a piece of art, you had to have a copyright notice on it. Films typically had a copyright notice on the titles, which ensured that the right people had the copyright and got paid.

The distributor of *Night of the Living Dead* made a small change, which ended up putting the film into the public domain.

The distributor the original title of the film *Night of the Flesh Eaters*, to *Night of the Living Dead*. When they changed the title, they didn't put the copyright notice back on the film and that removed all copyright protections from the film.

The distributors still got their take from the movie, but the writers and director never did. The film has ended up making as much as $42 million since then.

Anyone can make a copy of *Night of the Living Dead*. It's freely available all over the Internet and no one makes money off it, since it's a public-domain film. This is all due to one simple mistake.

The copyright laws have been changed since then and it's much harder to make those types of mistakes, but you still need a good lawyer to make sure that everything's in order. *Night of the Living Dead* is one of the most influential films ever made and it embodies the dreams of most low-budget movie producers. It was made for barely any money, was full of independent spirit and it truly revolutionized the industry and, in particular, the horror genre. Inattention to detail on the part of a distributor took the financial potential away from the people who made the movie.

Note that the distributor still got *their* cut of the action.

Is Piracy a Threat?

The motion picture industry has its own copyright police. This organization advocates for creators in the firm industry. They represent US filmmakers at home and abroad and, in recent years, their job has become much more complicated. Here's something to keep in mind, however.

While piracy is not legal—or ethical—you may not have much to fear from it. The MPAA has released numbers on how much Hollywood has suffered at the hands of Internet piracy. Specifically, there is information that shows that piracy leads to increased sales, which may have something to do with a phenomenon that filmmakers understand intimately: buzz.

The contention over the research usually stems from the assumption that every instance of piracy equates to a sale that won't happen. This debate has been for years now, and not everyone agrees with the MPAA.

Some research has shown that, when something gets out in a pirated form, interest in it increases and, given that the pirated versions are never of the same quality as the legit versions, people who like the films go out and buy a legitimate copy. In essence, the pirated version of the film basically serves as the trailer for the legitimate version, persuading the viewer to go out and buy it.

There is sure to be more debate about this, but worrying about online piracy and copyright infringement may not be where you want to put your time and effort as a filmmaker. Your film, if it's interesting enough to the public, will get pirated, in all likelihood. It will get recorded on a camera in an international theater or it will get leaked from a screener, a DVD, a Blu-ray, or from some other source. You may not want to worry too much about this type of infringement and concentrate on making sure you're safe from having your intellectual property stolen from you by more familiar sources.

There are definitely things to be careful of that are rather new threats stemming from the Internet. Remember:

- *DVD screeners have to be kept out of the hands of potential leakers;*
- *Scripts and shooting schedules can be stolen and leaked online;*
- *Notes from meetings are sometimes leaked;*
- *Recordings made on cell phones during the production process may be leaked to the detriment of the movie.*

In all likelihood, piracy won't cut into your profits much and your entertainment lawyer will make sure that all your rights are secured. If you're in doubt about contracts with foreign distributors, make sure your attorneys are experienced with the laws of that nation or that they have contacts in that nation who can provide assistance.

One Final Word: Conflict of Interest

It's been said before in this book and in many other places: the film business is built on personal networks. Sometimes, those personal networks may work against you.

Whenever you're seeking any type of legal representation to secure your rights or to represent you in court, be sure there's not a conflict of interest that you have to take into account. An attorney that you hire may end up having done a lot of business for someone attached to the party you're in conflict with, and that may go against you if it comes to some sort of a heated dispute.

Be sure that anyone you hire works for you and you alone. as an example, if you're working out a contract with an actor using an attorney that's worked for that actor in the past, you might have a problem getting the best deal. It's not that the attorney will try to cheat you, but they may not be as aggressive when negotiating against someone that they know personally and may even call a friend.

References:

http://www.wipo.int/about-ip/en/iprm/

http://www.americanbar.org/cle/cle_courses_by_topic/entertainment_law.html

http://www.wipo.int/export/sites/www/freepublications/en/intproperty/450/wipo_pub_450.pdf

http://www.hollywoodreporter.com/thr-esq/screenwriter-sues-disneypixar-claiming-cars-169543

http://www.westegg.com/inflation/infl.cgi

http://www.imdb.com/title/tt0063350/faq

http://www.plagiarismtoday.com/2011/10/10/how-a-copyright-mistake-created-the-modern-zombie/

http://www.gao.gov/products/GAO-10-423

http://www.mpaa.org/contentprotection/copyright-laws

http://www.nytimes.com/2004/07/19/technology/19piracy.html?ex=1247976000&en=2ddf51ee027bf359&ei=5090&partner=techdirt

Chapter 10

Marketing Ideas for a Digital Age

Marketing is serious work and producers sometimes play a part in it, particularly when a movie is being shopped around for distribution or reviews. Even though it is serious work, the type of creative people who work in Hollywood have also engaged in some of the cleverest marketing imaginable and some of it succeeded in making a film memorable. A good producer trying to generate interest in their film can do the same.

Getting the Buzz Out, Literally

William Castle is remembered as one of the best of the best where creating hype for a film is concerned. He produced and directed the 1959 film , starring Vincent Price. The film is the epitome of '50s schlock; featuring a centipede/earwig type rubber monster that's supposed to kill people when they get scared, but fail to scream. It kills by sheer terror, basically.

In some of the theater seats where the movie was shown, Castle primed the crowd with an announcement at the beginning of the film that some members of the audience might feel the presence of the

Tingler. This was called "Percepto" by Castle. In one scene, Vincent Price cries that the Tingler has gotten loose in the theater and that everyone needs to scream for their lives. The seats start buzzing at this point, no doubt sending their occupants into a screaming fit and people hired by Castle throughout the theater started screaming on cue.

This was clever marketing and the fact that people still remember it as a clever way to get notoriety for a film over 50 years after its release is telling. Today, a good producer can do much more than this, and the Internet, rather than seat buzzers, makes it possible.

Here are some ways that you can publicize a film and reach out to new audiences that may not have heard of it otherwise, particularly if the distribution that you want doesn't come through. Even if a studio has decided to put a lacking effort behind promoting a film, the producer and others involved and still do a lot, provided it's within their rights to do so under the contracts that apply to the film.

Social Media
Social media can be used to create buzz about films. This can be done using Twitter, Facebook or any of the other sites out there.

There is ample information available about promoting business ventures on Facebook. Much of the procedure will apply to films and, importantly, Facebook is about getting user engagement via posts, which should typically be newsworthy. Facebook, like the world of filmmaking, is also about exploiting personal networks, and consider doing so if you're on the system.

For example, actors and actresses typically have Facebook pages. As much as you can allow them to do so without leaking information about the film, allow them to post updates on the set and with other information. This helps to promote the film to their followers, which can get people interested. Remember that this can be useful when you're looking at distribution deals, as you can already point to a lot of interest among people.

Twitter is more oriented to news than Facebook is. Twitter limits the characters you can send out, so short and sweet is the order of the day.

Twitter happens to be very popular with celebrities. Many celebrity fights are had out on Twitter and it's one of the places that the media tend to check when they're looking for information on a movie, a TV show, or a given celebrity. Network with your stars and, if they have followers, their followers will get more exposures to your movie, increasing awareness that it's out there, or that it will be soon.

Movie Websites

Producers likely spend a lot of time on these sites themselves, which include those that are specifically designed to cater to the film fan and filmmaker crowd.

Advertising on these sites may be beneficial, if it's within the budget. Getting featured on one of these sites may be priceless.

IMDb.com is a very wide-ranging movie site that covers theatrical releases, DVD releases and industry news. It has extensive trailers and cast and crew information for a huge number of films. In reality, this site delivers on its promise, which is to be the Internet Movie Database. IMDb Pro is used by industry players and can be a tremendous resource for getting information on people in the film industry.

Yahoo! Movies is a news and reviews site with some basic industry information. That said, people love it and it's extremely popular. It is aimed at consumers and everyday moviegoers more than the connoisseur crowd that will to find IMDb preferable. Photos and trailers are available on this site.

Rotten Tomatoes is an aggregate review site with plenty of additional features. It features reviews of new releases by the top critics in the nation, as well as reviews by people who don't have much weight behind their opinions. Rotten Tomatoes features trailers, photos, and plenty of other content. It's a good site for finding out what's hot and whether or not the films live up to the hype that the studios given them.

One great thing to keep in mind about Rotten Tomatoes is that it gives ratings from critics and the audience. For example, two days after its November 27, 2013 release, the Jason Statham vehicle *Homefront* had a rating of 32% from critics, which may lead one to believe that it was headed for a complete flop. Audiences gave it a 70% approval rating. On Rotten Tomatoes, if the critics hate your film, the audience can make sure that they get a chance to contradict the bad reviews.

Sites for the Film

Another option to consider is building a website specifically for the film. This is almost a given for any Hollywood film these days and the sites are usually geared toward the complete sales process.

They get the viewer interested with images and trailers. They usually have a community of some sort set up on them, where the fans can talk to one another and pump each other up about going to see the movie.

The site will usually go right to the ticket sale, so fans have a one-stop destination for getting information and buying a ticket. If your film is already being distributed, these sites can be linked up with any of the major sites where people buy movies, such as Fandango.

Look at the site for the franchise to get an idea of what these sites look like. Even before a film is released, there may be a site set up for it and there is sometimes a great deal of activity on the site, increasing the buzz for the film. Look at these sites for films slated for 2015, to get an idea of how this type of marketing can work for a film.

Building a site is a great way to get a bit of message control over what goes on with fan speculation about a film. The director, producer and other high-ups can participate from time to time, increasing interest in the film by giving out clues as to what's to come.

In the event that the film has already been released, websites that advertise it can still be useful for fan engagement. When films are a bit heady and the audience may have many different ideas as to what the film meant or what went on in the film, the sites are great places for them to debate. With a writer, producer or director throwing out some information to keep everyone talking, they can become great places for fans to gather.

Conventions

Conventions—oftentimes called cons—are great places to market movies. Particularly if the movie very much fits in a given niche, there is probably a convention for it.

In the US, comic book conventions are great marketing opportunities. Dragon Con in Atlanta, GA and the San Diego Comic-Con International—usually called Comic Con—are good examples. These are commonly venues where movies and television shows are promoted and they can cross many different genres. Superhero movies are obviously big with this crowd, but sci-fi, horror and drama also resonate well with them and these can be great places to get word out about a film.

The largest conventions may be out of the price range of a small-budget film for promotional purposes. The smaller conventions can be equally useful.

In addition to the comic book conventions, there are actual horror conventions, sci-fi conventions, and so forth. These can be good places to get the word out . Most cities have these at least once a year and showing the film or having a booth can be great ways to get fans interested and possibly make the film more attractive to distributors or boost sales.

Some of these conventions are absolute media frenzies, which makes it worth participation. With some random press coverage, it might be passage to get a lot of people interested in a film and to get people in the seats to see it when it comes to town.

Be Creative

There are plenty of ways to market films that were not even accessible before. Everything from working conventions and film festivals, to getting a tie-in with a video game is a real possibility.It can make a film much more successful than its budget might have allowed if it were only promoted in the most conventional methods.

References:

http://www.ebizmba.com/articles/movie-websites

http://www.ebizmba.com/articles/movie-websites

http://www.imdb.com/

http://www.movies.yahoo.com/

http://www.rottentomatoes.com

http://www.thehungergamesexplorer.com/us/epk/hunger-games//

Conclusion

Making a film is a long, arduous process. It requires a very large crew, even for a low-budget film. It means working with unions and contracts, getting locations set up, finding the right director, actors, and more. It means working in a distribution industry that stacks everything against low-budget producers and that is full of ways for people to end up not getting their fair share of the profits from the art that they created.

From a production standpoint, the things that make a movie work include organization, a commitment to staying within the given budget, solid decisions in terms of hiring a director and actors and, a good concept, well executed by the script. Without these things, the film will doomed.

When it's time to get the film out there into theaters, the producer has to make sure that it is advertised properly, that the right people get to see it, and that everything is secured in terms of intellectual property rights so that no one is cheated out of what they are owed.

Working the film festival circuit can be as complex as producing the movie, with thousands of films being sent in for consideration, a small fraction of them being shown and a smaller fraction of those chosen being memorable for the audience.

As the producer, about everything is against you, but this is why some people cannot resist this job.

Being the producer means making it happen. It means facilitating the visions of the writer, the actors, and the director. It means putting to the greatest use the skills of lighting experts, costumers, and CGI experts. It means taking their work and marketing it to an industry that is always ready for the next big thing, but that oftentimes forgets to look at the next *best* thing.

When a producer meets all of these challenges, the results can be incredible artistically and commercially. Low-budget films can be hugely successful and launch the careers of truly gifted people.

Low-budgets films do matter in a world where blockbusters get all the credit. With a good producer, those low-budget films can launch genres, and the producer is there to make sure that small—but important—details, such as getting the rights secured, are taken care of. Without the producer, many an artistic vision will never be made into a great film, and the film industry would not be the success that it is today.

Photo Credits

In order of appearance:

http://commons.wikimedia.org/wiki/File:Filmaufnahmen_Radio_Bremen_-_Restaurant_Grissini,_Muenchen,_Oktober_2007.jpg

http://commons.wikimedia.org/wiki/File:JoyceUlysses2.jpg

http://commons.wikimedia.org/wiki/File:Tournage_du_documentaire_%22Les_Astres_Errants%22_%C3%A0_l%27observatoire_de_la_Silla_au_Chili.JPG

Shaka from It http://commons.wikimedia.org/wiki/File:Ciak.jpg

http://commons.wikimedia.org/wiki/File:Red_One_MX.jpg

http://commons.wikimedia.org/wiki/File:Bounce_Board,_by_Brian_Finifter.jpg

http://commons.wikimedia.org/wiki/File:Audiovisualstudio.jpg

http://commons.wikimedia.org/wiki/File:DVD-R_bottom-side.jpg

http://commons.wikimedia.org/wiki/File:Green_screen.jpg

Kevin Thompson
http://commons.wikimedia.org/wiki/File:Sundance_classic.jpg

All photos are licensed under Creative Commons and free to share and remix as long as the new product is also made available to share alike.

www.ingramcontent.com/pod-product-compliance
Lightning Source LLC
LaVergne TN
LVHW051832080426
835512LV00018B/2833